CW00554356

A View from the Wings

The author's arrival at the Fairey Company coincided with this style of early 1950s advertising. (Fairey Archive)

A View from the Wings

60 Years in Aviation

Colin Cruddas

The History Press

Every effort has been made to contact the copyright holders of images included in this publication. Any errors will be rectified in future editions.

Cover images: *Front, top to bottom*: Fairey Rotodyne, Concorde and Hawker Siddeley (Blackburn) Buccaneer. *Back*: The Blackburn Company gates at Brough. (Blackburn Archive)

First published 2012

The History Press
The Mill, Brimscombe Port
Stroud, Gloucestershire, GL5 2QG
www.thehistorypress.co.uk

© Colin Cruddas, 2012

The right of Colin Cruddas to be identified as the Author of this work has been asserted in accordance with the Copyrights, Designs and Patents Act 1988.

All rights reserved. No part of this book may be reprinted or reproduced or utilised in any form or by any electronic, mechanical or other means, now known or hereafter invented, including photocopying and recording, or in any information storage or retrieval system, without the permission in writing from the Publishers.

British Library Cataloguing in Publication Data.
A catalogue record for this book is available from the British Library.

ISBN 978 0 7524 7748 0

Typesetting and origination by The History Press
Printed in Great Britain

CONTENTS

FOREWORD

By Sir Michael Knight KCB AFC FRAeS

This is a very readable and remarkably detailed account of the author's life and career in the aerospace industry, where he plied his trade in the UK, USA, South Africa and, from time to time, even further afield. A proud Yorkshire lad, he was born and brought up in Bridlington – not a place generally associated with aviation but which certainly saw its share of the action, both 'ours' and 'theirs', during the Second World War; and which, clearly, was then a happy hunting ground for a young and enquiring adolescent. And it was this which, perhaps inevitably, played a key part in inspiring the young Cruddas to embark on what was to become a lifetime in and around his chosen profession.

Entering the aircraft industrial scene as an 18-year-old trainee draughtsman with the Fairey Aviation Company, his burgeoning career later took him to the Blackburn (Hawker Siddeley), Boeing, McDonnell Douglas, British Aircraft Corporation and Atlas companies, before his final return to the UK with Flight Refuelling Limited. It was in the latter post that a major health problem brought an early retirement but also, in due course, a second career as the successful author of a range of books on the history and development of aviation in Britain. His long and varied engineering and administrative experience on a wide variety of aircraft, from Gannet to Concorde and beyond, makes this a fascinating volume – particularly for those with an interest in the last sixty or so turbulent years of a great British industry.

In this, his first autobiographical work, the author writes well in a style which manages to balance a wealth of technical detail with many humorous and engagingly self-deprecating anecdotes. A very good read indeed!

Michael Knight

Fairey Aviation displays its latest asset at the Society of British Aircraft Constructors exhibition at Farnborough in 1952. The Firefly looks pretty good as well!

ACKNOWLEDGEMENTS & DEDICATION

W hat follows required an energetic spring clean of my memory department, along with a fair amount of supporting research. There have, however, been many areas where I have needed to sharpen up on detail and I have been extremely fortunate in being able to call up 'air support' from several long-term and new-found friends. Accordingly, my most sincere thanks go to Aimee and Harry Alexander (Poole Flying Boats Celebration), Ken Baillie (ex-Fairey Aviation and British Aircraft Corporation colleague), Roger Bellamy (ex-RAF Old Sarum colleague), Paul Bright (Yorkshire aviation author), Dudley Dobson (ex-East Lancashire Coachbuilding Company and contemporary apprentice), Brian Gardner (aviation author and historian), Colin van Geffen (aviation author, artist and Fawley historian), David Gibbings (ex-Fairey Aviation and AgustaWestland archivist and author), Bryan Hope (ex-Fairey Aviation and drawing office school colleague), Squadron Leader Tony Iveson DFC (ex-617 Squadron and vice president of the Bomber Command Association), David Neave (University of Hull and Bridlington historian and author), Norman Parker (ex-Vickers Armstrong, Fairey Aviation and aviation historian), Mike Phipp (Bournemouth Airport historian and aviation author), Ted Talbot (ex-British Aircraft Corporation colleague and aviation author), the late Terry Waddington (ex-Blackburn Aircraft, McDonnell Douglas Aircraft historian, aviation author and Bridlington boyhood pal) and David Wright (ex-RAF 1104 Marine Craft Unit and Bridlington boyhood pal). Whew! It's quite a list. I wouldn't have got far without them.

The BAE Systems Heritage Centres at both Brough (Eric Barker, Paul Lawson and Peter Hotham) and Warton (Keith Spong and Tom Clayton) have willingly provided keen co-operation in supplying photographs, for which I am most grateful.

Bridlington's ever enthusiastic and knowledgeable historian David Mooney has played a key part in this work and deserves a very special mention for providing local material and facts that had either slipped my memory or, in many cases, I simply wasn't aware of.

I also wish to include at this point Air Chief Marshal Sir Michael Knight KBE AFC FRAeS, who, in responding to my appeal as an ex-Cobham plc and Buccaneer Aircrew Association colleague, instantly and kindly agreed to provide a foreword to this book. (I doubt I would have made such a presumptuous request to a high-ranking officer in my National Service days, but time has now, fortunately, eased some of the protocol boundaries.)

One of the pleasures of putting together a book of this nature is the making of new contacts and friendships. Rick Phillips, incidentally the only man ever to fly a Buccaneer, XV 168, (now the gate guardian) into Brough, who kindly checked over my Fairey and Blackburn references for service accuracy, and Dave Herriot, both of the Buccaneer Aircrew Association, certainly fall into this category. So, too, do Sarah Hutchinson and her colleagues at the Bridlington Public Library and the East Riding of Yorkshire County Council for having made available pictures of The Spa in Bridlington and those showing wartime damage in the town.

In some instances I have been unable to track down the original sources of illustration material, so I do ask those people for their forgiveness. I realise how annoying and seemingly ungrateful it can be when one's work appears elsewhere without proper accreditation, so I thank you. It almost goes without saying that The History Press, with Abbie Wood leading the production team, has done its usual highly professional job and, as on so many earlier projects, it has been my great pleasure to work with them on this volume.

Finally, hoping that I haven't left any key contributors out, I must express deep gratitude to my wife Thelma, who has contributed to the onerous task of proofreading, and, to use her chilling phrase, 'tightened things up' when far higher priorities (e.g. the garden or meal preparations) arose. Our younger daughter Sally has shown immense patience when frequently bailing me out of computer glitches, mainly of my own making, and I can't thank her enough for that.

Having now produced over a dozen or so works on specialist aviation topics, this one, I believe, is best suited for dedication to 'the family'. So to Thelma, Helen and Sally, along with their families – Jennifer, Jonathan, Angus, Giles and Robert – and not forgetting our mothers, both called May, who after all placed us on life's path, this is for you.

INTRODUCTION

This book is the result of persistent persuasion by our elder daughter Helen, who thinks that after a long life of largely undetected crime, mine might be a tale worth telling. Hopefully, both she and her sister Sally will be proved right, but you, dear reader, will have to be the final judge of that.

Life, we know, is full of challenges and frustrations, a fact quickly affirmed when I began searching for a suitable title. Dr Stanley Hooker, after retiring in 1984 as Rolls-Royce's technical director, published his autobiography with the tongue-in-cheek title of *Not Much of an Engineer*. Everyone in the aerospace world knew that this hardly accorded with his reputation as one of Britain's best aeronautical engineers. I, on the other hand, while admiring the cleverness of his choice, felt I could have claimed his self-effacing title with far more justification and with no false modesty whatsoever.

Thus forestalled, it was back to the drawing board for a title which adequately described my involvement with so many aerospace projects over the last half of the twentieth century. My lifetime's technical contribution made, I admit, little serious impact on aviation's progress, but it has been my great privilege to work alongside some highly talented engineers, designers and aircrew whose efforts certainly did provide a way forward. So, perhaps my choice of *A View from the Wings* best describes these career recollections, which, seasoned with some of a more general nature, should spark memories of the days when Britain had an industry that actually produced *complete aeroplanes*. Cricket, being my other love, has also somehow forced its way into my story.

1

'BRID KID' BEGINNINGS

More than sixty years ago (when this tale begins), on a grey Saturday morning in late March 1951, I set out just days after my eighteenth birthday in a belted raincoat, trilby hat perched jauntily on my head, with a student-sized T-square strapped to the side of my canvas suitcase. I was going on a steam train journey south, from Bridlington on the Yorkshire coast to Hayes in Middlesex. Here, a new life as a trainee draughtsman at the Fairey Aviation Company beckoned. A quick backward glance confirmed that my mother was watching my departure, no doubt with a misty eye from behind a barely parted curtain in the bay window of 9 St John's Walk. Spurred on by youthful enthusiasm, my main concern at that moment was not so much with leaving home as possibly missing the train. What, one might ask, had brought about such an adventurous move?

In the post-war period, life in my home town was much dictated by one's social circumstances; in other words, the local 'well-to-do' continued to do what they had always done regarding the management of local affairs. Bridlington's town council and the trading

Goodbye to all that. St John's Walk in Bridlington today, showing sixty years of wear and tear since I last lived there. No 9 is the fifth house from the left.

community, ever mindful of the competition offered by Scarborough just 18 miles up the coast, were strongly determined to rebuild the town's pre-war reputation as a wholesome family holiday resort and ideal seaside retirement centre. 'Scarborough? Much colder up there and far too hilly for older folk' might well have underlined 'Bright, Breezy, Bridlington' as the town's favourite advertising slogan. This approach, though understandable, resulted in worthwhile employment opportunities remaining limited. An attempt in 1947 to introduce light industry appeared promising when the East Lancashire Coachbuilding Company, albeit with its major factory and headquarters over the Pennines in Blackburn, established an assembly plant on the new Bessingby Industrial Estate. But despite this progressive move, local people instinctively knew their place in what was, until the sixties, generally accepted as 'the British way of life'. At that time, Bridlington's fishing industry and the provision of visitor accommodation and entertainment sat comfortably alongside an agricultural community that did not want to see the town become an industrial extension of the West Riding. Most people with 'professional' aspirations were to be found in the same seat in the same carriage on the same early morning train to either Beverley or Hull – in all probability, much like those of today.

My mother, May, while possessing an amiable but reserved personality, always ensured she was suitably deferential to the ladies who patronised The Lounge restaurant and cake shop on Bridlington's Promenade. It was there, in what was still the town's highest-class watering hole, though struggling to recover its genteel pre-war Palm Court ambience, that she was employed as manageress and cashier for the adjoining cinema in the evening.

Left: My mother, Edna May, *c.* 1950.

Below: With grandma on Bridlington's Esplanade in 1938.

Prior to her engagement at The Lounge she had worked at the Oberon cake shop in Queen Street, and before that at Wade's Chapel Street shoe shop. However, it was after returning home from the Wade family's Selby store in 1932 that May discovered she was pregnant. Not a good situation; not good at all. Marriage, she told me in a rare confiding moment years later, was not an option, though she did add that the contributing gentleman's name was Norman Featherstone and that he was much younger. Armed with only this minimal amount of information regarding my father, I found subsequent attempts to gain further clarification either from her or from other relatives always ended with a shake of the head.

In those pre-war days, and indeed for many years after the war, a single parent condition, though by no means uncommon, was almost regarded as a hanging offence and I'm certain the guilt and sense of shame it incurred remained with my mother to the end of her days. At the time, this social impediment had little impact on me for until my early teens I was brought up to believe that May was my sister, who simply went out to work every day, and that my grandmother Alice, who looked after me with great affection, was my mother. In later years I was most surprised to find that even the famous Hollywood actor Jack Nicholson had laboured under an almost identical delusion until his adulthood. Although this caused me no emotional hang-ups, I must admit it did come as something of a shock to find at age 14, just after my grandmother's death in 1947, that my family's relationships were not as I had always believed. I then found it impossible – until much later in life – to call my 'newly appointed' birth mother anything but May. My efforts at calling her Mum always seemed awkward and I have little doubt that she had similar difficulties adjusting to her changed role.

Grandad Robert, a private in the Army Service Corps during the First World War, and grandma Alice caught in thoughtful mood.

My great-grandmother Elizabeth Anne, who died, aged 84, in 1937. She lost three sons in the First World War and her husband, Thomas Cruddas, in the influenza pandemic just after the war ended.

I might add that this arrangement would have been impossible to maintain had my grandfather, Robert, been alive. Tragically, after serving in the First World War in France, Egypt, Palestine and then France again, he, along with five others, was killed while attached to the 231st Field Ambulance Unit when a German shell struck their dugout on 30 October 1918. With the end of the war less than two weeks away, his death, following that of two of his brothers, must have been an unimaginable loss for my great-grandmother, who saw her husband die in the Spanish influenza pandemic less than a year later. The net result of this family decimation was that Alice, then living at 36 Brookland Road, was left to bring up four children – Catherine, Bobby, Harold and May – throughout the 1920s. And to complicate matters further, I arrived.

I was born on 28 February 1933 at St Oswald's Nursing Home in Bridlington, which incidentally took place within a few hours of the burning down of the Reichstag in Berlin. Though both events were clearly momentous, my impact on the world has hardly matched that of Adolf Hitler, but I can at least boast that I have lasted considerably longer. Besides that, I think I turned out to be a much more approachable sort of chap, not given to pulling my hair out (despite constant provocation by my computer), biting the carpet or indulging in any other irritating tantrums attributed to the German leader.

My pre-war boyhood was pleasantly unremarkable with no school-related traumas that I can recall. Being a seaside resort, Bridlington had its fair share of gala events, often featuring the orchestras of Herman Darewski and Lionel Johns, whose concert nights at The Spa and the Floral Hall on the Esplanade, along with firework displays over The Spa boating lake, I can still faintly remember. Also within my pre-war recall is what I regard as my first aeronautical memory, but being only 4½ years old at the time the significance of the event literally passed over me. I had caught a very brief glimpse of the Imperial Airways Short S.23 C-Class flying boat G-ADHM *Caledonia* as it flew over the town as part of a Round Britain tour on 30 August 1937. My view of this aerial wonder as it flitted between the chimney pots can have lasted but a few seconds, but it formed the first never-to-be-forgotten aviation image in my young, impressionable mind.

Right: Herman Darewski, who first appeared in Bridlington in 1936, was the first bandleader to introduce dances at The Spa that went beyond 9 p.m. It was later alleged that the Luftwaffe pilot who accurately bombed Bridlington's railway station had been a member of Darewski's pre-war orchestra and knew the town well. There's gratitude for you! (*The Spa: Bridlington*, 2008)

Below: Imperial Airways quickly lost a number of its Empire C Class flying boats following their introduction into service. *Caledonia* made a round-Britain tour, flying over Bridlington in 1937, to encourage public confidence. (Poole Flying Boat Celebration)

When war was declared in September 1939, it wasn't long before lads of my tender vintage became aware that exciting times were now upon us. At least that was what our parents told us. Despite the issue of gas masks to everyone, public shelters appearing and walls of sandbags being formed in front of local buildings such as the schools and the town hall, life just carried on as normal. It all seemed a bit of an anticlimax and even our elders wondered what all the fuss was about. It was not until after the German advance into Western Europe in May 1940, after a truly cold winter, that things really started to heat up. Now aged 7, I made my contribution to Britain's wartime effort by following the Wehrmacht's advances in the *Daily Express*; with a bit of adult assistance I would plot the changes in the Allies' front line with small paper flags, bearing either the swastika or a Union Jack, on a large map supplied by the newspaper. Each evening, the Ekco Bakelite-encased radio would slowly crackle into life, just in time for Alvar Liddell to sonorously announce, through the usual atmospheric crackle: 'This is the BBC Home Service. Here is the news. Today saw German forces moving forward on a wide front ...' Such, however, was the daily rate of the Nazi advance and the British retreat to Dunkirk, that I soon became adept at moving both lines of flags back towards the French coast, just like the opening graphics of *Dad's Army*.

Though usually hustled off to bed soon afterwards, I always left the bedroom door open in order to hear snatches of Tommy Handley in *ITMA* (*It's That Man Again*) or the droll Liverpudlian comedian Rob Wilton, recounting: 'The day war broke out, my missus said to me, what are you going to do about it?' Another favourite was *Big Bill Campbell and his Rocky Mountaineers*, who were forever having their Canadian bunkhouse door blown open and then slammed shut against a snowy blizzard by some wandering artiste keen to render a song. 'Mighty fine, mighty fine!' Big Bill would invariably intone after each number, just before the door swooshed open again to admit the next performer who just happened to be passing by. There must have been a queue a mile long of ice-encrusted 'strangers' waiting to 'jus' drop in'. Well, at that age it all seemed real enough. However, I now imagine that Peggy, the 'Bunkhouse Sweetheart', raised morale as the troops let their sex-starved imaginations run riot.

As the Battle of Britain later began to rage, I patriotically ranged my Dinky Toy air force of less than a dozen Spitfires, Hurricanes and Gladiators against a handful of Whitley, Battle and Blenheim bombers, which in the absence of any corresponding German types had to serve as the enemy. My model Cierva Rota autogyro sat awkwardly in the midst of these confronting forces and then was cast aside for the remainder of the hostilities. Although at a loss to know how to accommodate this unconventional and ungainly bird into my imagined war scenarios, I later learned that a number were used to calibrate radar stations, such as those located on the nearby Bempton Cliffs and further up the coast at Staxton Wolds. Had I known this, I would willingly have included it in my air battle line-ups. Another addition to my Dinky Toy range was a Short Singapore Mk III biplane flying boat. Two of my friends, Bobby Mouncer and Lenny Aires, had the same model in their collections, so it was not unusual for the three of us to parade our silver flying boats in close formation up and down the street. It too, however, was not a type that fitted into the Britain versus Germany war game and had to be sidelined for the duration of the war. I hate to think of the price those Dinky Toy box wonders would bring today. Clearly, 'the air' was already beginning to occupy a large part of my imagination, further emphasised by my sitting huddled under a chair turned through 90° so that, with the chair legs parallel to the ground, I had a good approximation of a bomber's rear four-gun turret. Not many enemy fighters escaped my withering bursts, I can tell you!

Unaware of the deeper implications of the war news, I spent many happy hours in what we called Stabler's field behind our house with my immediate neighbouring pals, Dave

Wright and Brian Berkeley, and other kids like Fatty Snowden who lived nearby. When we weren't in the fields we were most likely playing cricket in the street, which with Victorian terraced houses on each side was very narrow. Play was interrupted every twenty minutes or so by the East Yorkshire double-decker bus passing by, but other road traffic was minimal and didn't affect the simple 'field placings' of 'get down't street as far as thee can'. What a contrast to today's congestion, with cars parked on both sides of the road; no room these days to swing a cat, let alone a cricket bat. Great reliance was placed on the pull shot, which supposedly despatched the ball to square leg, but in many cases catapulted it into somebody's prized front garden. All too often it went into Miss Lester's, a lady not noted for her tolerance of youthful behaviour, and we had to be in and out like greased lightning to retrieve the ball before she appeared, threatening to confiscate the ball.

The width of the road required anyone trying to bowl fast to run along the opposing pavement at right angles to the 'wicket', then stop and turn (all momentum lost, of course) to deliver a tennis ball to the batsman facing him some 12yd away. A well-delivered 'yorker' would often hit the facing edge of the kerb under the batsman's feet and bounce right back across the road, to provide a dubious 'caught and bowled'. This would be accompanied by expletives not entirely in keeping with the religious training I received each weekend at the Gospel Hall down the street. Such was the innocence of youth, I truly believed that my sawn-off relic of a bat, with the inscription 'Len Hutton, 364, The Oval, 1938' carved on the back, was indeed the one the Master had used to achieve his world test record score. It was one of life's first reality checks to discover that my cherished bat, with its 'three-springer' handle, was just a piece of lost property found on the beach by my Uncle Harold, its late owner most probably having been a day tripper from the West Riding. (Note: a 'three-springer' handle was supposed to imply that if turned upside down and dropped on to a hard surface – i.e. the pavement – the bat would bounce up and down three times. Mine never made it beyond one, but back then I had a simple belief in what I was told.)

'Bomber' was another St John's Walk pastime, wherein one of the kids hanging about was chosen to be a 'pilot' and told to run along the frontages of two adjacent houses while being pelted with tennis balls from the opposite pavement. It sounds innocuous enough, but we all had ferociously strong and accurate throws which guaranteed bruises galore on short-trousered boys' legs. Two hits and you were considered shot down, whereupon you thankfully retired to wreak equally painful revenge on the next brave soul. True to real life, running the first stage successfully only got one *to* the target; it was still necessary to do the return trip back to base. Oh, what painful fun!

Mention of the Gospel Hall brings to mind the tedious recitation of endless tracts of the Good Word, which meant little to me then and, I have to admit, even less to me now. Such perseverance was, however, rewarded with a Bible which might not have been so enthusiastically given had the preacher, 'Pop' Turner, realised that to relieve the sheer boredom of Sunday School I had earlier, and most surreptitiously, unscrewed the mushroom-shaped control wheels on the Hall's radiator valves for rolling down the road later on. With hindsight, this was a stupid thing to do, for apart from the inconvenience caused, wartime shortages meant that no replacements could be obtained. However, as no recriminations followed, I became emboldened enough to embark on another venture which certainly did cause me a bit of serious heart-searching. It all seems a non-event now, but I had taken up stamp collecting and found that a certain Mr Pinder's bric-a-brac stall in the town's Saturday market featured albums containing wonderful triangular stamps featuring aeroplanes, from exotic-sounding places like Liberia and Mozambique. Not that such places would be deemed particularly exotic today. These proved to be a temptation too far and while my grandma busied herself looking at Victorian knick-knacks, my furtive little hand was engaged in denuding album pages, well hidden so I thought under the one I was apparently studying. This seemingly easy way of enhancing one's own collection continued without mishap for a couple of weeks, until the dreaded day when the pork pie-hatted Mr Pinder grasped my arm.

'What have you got in your hand, son?' he enquired.

'Nothing,' said I, which was true, because in sheer fright I had dropped the goods enclosed in my fist. Seeing his wares fluttering to the ground, Mr Pinder released his grip to retrieve what he could before it floated away into the gutter. I floated away too, pretty damn fast, in the opposite direction, only to run into the arms of my grandma coming round the corner. Pleading instant illness and the urgent need for the toilet, an immediate confrontation was averted. But for weeks afterwards, as I lay each night in our Morrison steel-caged air-raid shelter, I suffered agonies, not at the thought of being bombed, but of being tracked down and placed behind more substantial bars to answer for my deed. Perhaps the most difficult part was passing, head down and keeping a very low and guilty profile, through 'enemy

'Pinderland' in Prince Street – not too different today, although the police car appears to have arrived seventy years too late!

territory' – i.e. 'Pinderland' – each subsequent weekend as grandma ritually examined the stall's offerings. My 'See you in Woollies [Woolworths] in ten minutes, Mam' was fortunately good enough to allay any suspicions as to my real motive for keeping well out of sight. As has often been suggested, a fatherly influence might, in those early years, have made a difference, but luckily for me this encounter brought sufficient distress to redirect me on to a more virtuous path.

Compared to the Luftwaffe raids on Hull, an hour's drive away, the thirty air attacks both during the day and night on Bridlington were relatively light. Most able-bodied folk were, nevertheless, required to 'do their bit', and by late 1940 my grandma was wearing a white-painted steel helmet when she went out at night on Air Raid Precautions duty. When I tried wearing it, I found I could turn nearly 90° without the helmet moving. May, too, put in a stint on the Auxiliary Fire Service telephone switchboard on her return from earning the daily bread, thus confirming Noel Coward's observation that 'They also serve, who only stand and faint – sorry, wait'.

For those unfortunate enough to be on the receiving end of a bomb, the consequences were, of course, devastating. Two of the main areas to suffer in Bridlington were Hilderthorpe Road and Prince Street, where the Cosy Corner Hotel, the Britannia Hotel, Woolworths and Foley's Cafe were either demolished or badly damaged. The pre-war pleasure steamer *Royal Sovereign* also received a direct hit at this time while moored in the harbour. As is often the case, there is always the 'first-hand' witness who saw the bomb 'go straight down the funnel' and I suppose I believed this to be true for many years, until I learnt the meaning of 'dramatic licence'. Bridlington's pleasure steamers certainly saw wartime life at the sharp end, for the original *Yorkshire Belle* also met a tragic end when it struck a magnetic mine in the Humber and was lost with all on board.

The intersection of Springfield Avenue and Hilderthorpe Road suffered damage that could have been intended for either the harbour or the railway station. The tall building in the background was the Cosy Corner Hotel (now The Coachman). (East Riding of Yorkshire County Council)

Prince Street saw
Woolworths,
Foley's Cafe and
the Britannia
Hotel blasted by
enemy bombs
within days
of the attack
on Driffield
aerodrome.
(Bridlington
Public Library)

I didn't think too deeply at the time of my mother's fanciful 'combat account' in which she claimed to have seen a German bomber flying so low over the main Quay Road railway crossing that she could see the pilot waving. Sadly, she is no longer with us for me to better establish the facts, but I have no doubt that, stripped of any embellishments, she certainly did witness a low-level attack on the railway station.

Other raids brought about the destruction of the post office, the local electricity board showrooms on Quay Road and St George's School, which lost its assembly hall and gymnasium. In what was considered at the time to be a remarkable pin-point attack, a wagon loaded with ammunition in the railway station sidings received a lucky direct hit, thus ensuring that things went off with a bang on that particular morning. I believe this was the event described by my mother.

It was following these attacks that Tom Hopper Alderson became the first recipient of the George Cross (the civilian equivalent of the Victoria Cross) for his bravery in the town's rescue operations. It was later alleged that a member of Herman Darewski's popular band (some reports said it was his brother) was a pilot in the attacks on Bridlington and that orders had been given to avoid bombing The Spa in case Darewski was still playing there. Despite the name Herman suggesting German origins, the fact that Darewski was born in Russia hardly supported such a consideration.

It was also rumoured that Sewerby Hall, a favourite country house and gardens attraction some 2 miles north of the town, was deliberately spared by the Luftwaffe because Hitler had expressed a desire to live there after the German invasion. There *may* be some truth in the Darewski story, but I suspect that Hitler's preference for Sewerby Hall was the figment of local imagination and can be safely consigned to the 'legend has it' bin.

There was some genuine excitement one day when a Junkers 88 A-4, 4D-DR of 7.KG 30 was brought down by Sergeant Jim Hopewell, flying a 616 Squadron Spitfire, around 3 miles

This Ju 88 A-4, 4D-DR, was brought down on 15 August 1940 by Sergeant Jim Hopewell of 616 Squadron, close to Bridlington's water reservoir on Scarborough Road.

outside Bridlington along the Scarborough Road. This took place on 15 August 1940, the Luftwaffe's *Adlertag* (Eagle Day), when a bomber force of Ju 88s attacked the RAF's Driffield aerodrome 12 miles south-west of Bridlington. I remember distinctly the day being overcast and walking with my (real) mother in the fields behind our house; we heard this unusual engine noise above the clouds as the aircraft lined up to bomb the airfield. Not that anyone knew it at the time, but this turned out to be the heaviest raid on a British bomber station throughout the entire war. Considerable damage was caused, with four out of five hangars and various mess buildings being virtually destroyed; also, ten Whitley bombers, five each from Nos 77 and 102 Squadrons, were written off and others seriously damaged. Fourteen military and civilian lives were also lost. It was some consolation that twelve 616 Squadron Spitfires from Leconfield and six 73 Squadron Hurricanes from Church Fenton (detached to Leconfield) ensured that eleven out of the enemy's final force of seventeen (though numbers do vary considerably according to source) failed to make it back to their base at Aalborg in Denmark. For a detailed account of this event and also the part played by the East Riding in the air war, see Paul Bright's book, *The Air War Over East Yorkshire in World War II*, which is excellent.

Perhaps the most bizarre event on that dreadful day at Driffield was the sparing of an airman's life while he was under arrest in the guardroom. The story goes that this airframe fitter had earlier decided to take off alone in a visiting Fairey Battle for a local 'joyride'. Taken into custody after landing, he apparently walked out of the guardroom without a

The RAF adopted rigid battle formations at the start of the war. My outstanding memory of this was seeing a squadron of Hurricanes patrolling over Bridlington Bay one fine Sunday morning. Sensing imminent trouble, and braving the piecing noise of the air-raid warning siren on top of Lloyds Bank in Manor Street (it's still there), I scooted for home in record time.

scratch after it was flattened in the attack. Close escapes during the war have, of course, been recorded at endless length in many other books, but in mentioning the Driffield guardroom incident, I'm mindful of how good or bad fortune was forever 'just around the corner'.

Weather forecasting at this time was a notoriously unreliable business, and coupled with limited navigational aids made bombing raids in the early part of the war a distinctly hit or miss affair. According to my wartime pilot friend Peter French (see Appendix II), a serious navigational error nearly brought about one of the RAF's worst wartime 'own goals'. This resulted from a faulty weather forecast, which indicated a 70mph wind blowing from the north when in fact it was blowing from the south. The experienced Canadian pilot of a Stirling bomber, briefed to attack a target near Calais, was blown well off course and mistook the Thames Estuary for the English Channel. After returning to base, interrogation of the navigator and skipper revealed that the Stirling, far from dropping its bombs on France, had in fact unloaded its full cargo of 32 x 500lb bombs in a straight line across the Kent countryside near Canterbury. Fortunately, no one was killed and no extensive damage caused, but imagine the furore that would have ensued had the cathedral been demolished. The whole incident was hushed up and the crew concerned split up and posted away from the squadron. According to Peter, there were other incidents which proved costly to the war effort. One of the most serious was the failure of bombs to explode after so many lives and aircraft had been lost while delivering them. It was later discovered that although the explosive material within the bombs was highly stable, the chemicals used in the detonators was relatively unstable and degraded over time. Some of the detonators used early in the war had been in store for years and by 1939 had become 'stale', so to speak, hence their unreliability. The learning curve was indeed a steep one!

Returning to more personal matters, I did not actually see the aeroplane brought down on Scarborough Road, but my reliable Uncle Harold managed to 'acquire' from it a Werke number plate and a system component which emitted such a strong smell of hydraulic oil that it was not allowed indoors. Its immediate disposal meant that I missed out on a good trading opportunity with my school friends.

In parallel with the enemy's comings and goings over Bridlington, which had little strategic significance, the docks at Hull took a terrific pasting in what became nationally referred to as 'The Blitz'. It was always a source of immense local irritation when BBC announcements used the general description 'in the north-east' following attacks by the Luftwaffe, while southern towns and cities received first-hand recognition. It is no exaggeration to say that this was, for many northern folk, a very sensitive issue. Not, of course, that one would admit such unworthy observations to a southerner; one does have one's pride, but 'by 'eck, they've damn well done it again. No mention of 'ull on't news this mornin'. Are we in't bloody war or what?' A good question, too, thought many, forlornly surveying the debris still smoking from the previous night's raid. Little was it known at the time, but such was the extent of devastation in the city that official censorship prohibited specific reference to Hull and insisted on 'a north-east town' in announcements as the best alternative likely to confuse German intelligence. So many statements made back then are now almost impossible to corroborate, but one which stated that in terms of high explosives delivered per capita, Bridlington, with a wartime population of around 19,000, received the highest proportion in the country may well be true. Nevertheless, I believe Great Yarmouth, which experienced some ninety attacks, laid justifiable claim to the same distinction. With enemy aircraft using Flamborough Head as a main navigational landmark en route to industrial centres in the Midlands, but finding their way blocked by fog or bad weather, it would have been a natural action for them to return along the same path, jettisoning their bomb loads on to the last built-up area – Bridlington – before departing over the North Sea.

It was in the early morning of 19 March 1941 that my future wife Thelma Holbrook, then aged 6, emerged with her pregnant mother from one of Hull's shelters to find that their home at No 1 Carleton Avenue no longer existed. This was one of around 700 houses that were destroyed in that raid, the heaviest on the city. An official estimate stated that some 350 Junkers Ju 88s and Heinkel He 111s dropped over 300 tons of high-explosive bombs and 77,000 incendiaries during the attack. Further heavy raids throughout the war resulted in

A general plan showing the Yorkshire coastline.

Carleton Avenue in Hull, as it looked in the 1930s. It didn't look quite so ordered after a German bomb demolished No 1, the first house on the left and home to Thelma, my then 6-year-old wife to be. (Hull City Library)

half the population losing their homes. With husband and father away on military service, life for the Holbrook family, along with that of so many others, proved very hard indeed. Amazingly, a ceramic bowl and two of Thelma's mother's swimming prizes survived the devastation and remain today, cherished family items.

During the war, Thelma and her mother spent time with relatives in Hull and Bradford after being 'bombed out'. Fortunately for me, they finally became domiciled in Bridlington. This clearly proved, as I've pointed out so many times to Thelma's eye-rolling acceptance, that every cloud has a silver lining. Perhaps, on reflection, this analogy isn't all that appropriate, for, as once pointed out, the 'silver lining' could easily have been another aeroplane.

On 1 April 1941, 104 Squadron was re-formed at Driffield and Wellington bombers were introduced there. It must have been shortly after their arrival that through a coach window I saw for the first time an example of Bomber Command's early striking force. Not that at this time it was striking particularly hard or effectively. Lack of night-time pilot and navigational training, poor cockpit instrumentation and heating, along with 'dodgy' engine and airframe systems reliability, all contributed to a heavy loss of aircraft and crews beyond those caused by enemy action.

By 1942 I had developed a deep interest in aircraft. This was hardly surprising considering the enormous amount of local air activity, but also I had formed friendships with Jeff Brown and Pete Johnson who, being several years older than me, had influential contacts in the Royal Observer Corps. Though many types of aircraft were then in evidence, in the early war years they mainly consisted of twin-engined Whitleys, Hampdens, Blenheims and

The Vickers Armstrong Wellington was a familiar sight in Yorkshire skies and was the first aircraft I ever saw on the ground. This occurred during a coach 'mystery tour' with my grandma when passing RAF Driffield sometime before the ill-fated raid in August 1940.

Wellingtons; but later, the four-engined Halifax heavy bombers, flying from the bases at nearby Driffield, Leconfield and Lissett, dominated the skies. Nearby Catfoss, serving as 2 (Coastal) Operational Training Unit, also provided much in the way of training aircraft, ranging from the Miles Martinet to the Bristol Beaufighter, which until modifications to the tailplane was prone to crash at low speed. Not that I was then aware of such technical shortcomings, but I was certainly in no doubt as to the type, when one whistled by overhead.

Yorkshire and neighbouring Lincolnshire were effectively two enormous airfields with the approach circuits to so many bases virtually overlapping. Carnaby, situated just 2 miles south of Bridlington and which opened on 20 April 1944, played a vitally important part in the air war when it became one of fifteen emergency landing grounds round the country, equipped with FIDO (Fog Investigation and Dispersal Operation). I have seen minor variations to this acronym but believe this to be the official version. FIDO was a piping system which, with holes drilled along its length, ran along both sides of a vast runway. At Carnaby it was 250yd wide and 3,000yd long (five times the normal runway length). This arrangement allowed petrol vapour to rise and be burnt off, the resulting hot air lifting the all-too-frequent coastal mists to provide a clear approach for aircraft either badly damaged or simply lost. This may seem a simple solution, but in practice the installation problems proved formidable. The prioritising of wartime materials and skilled labour affected the supply and delivery of the necessary thousands of feet of piping and control components, plus the availability and billeting of welding and operating crews. Sustained operations required constant maintenance and it was not unusual to find long lengths of heat-distorted piping in need of total replacement.

The noise generated by the system was akin to a million painters' blowlamps, which once heard was never forgotten – and certainly not by those living nearby, when the first FIDO test was carried out, without public warning, in July 1944. Records show that in December 1944 – a month of bitter, freezing fog – Carnaby accommodated 228 emergency landings, including sixty-five that required the assistance of FIDO and a demand for some 1.7 million gallons of petrol.

As an 11-year-old I well remember hearing, in the persistent, swirling murk of 31 January 1945, the sound of FIDO at full blast. Operating between 0945 and 1550 hours, the system consumed 114,000 gallons of petrol in facilitating the safe landing not only of six non-operational Halifaxes caught out on exercises, but sixty-five USAAF 2nd Air Division B-24 Liberator bombers, returning from an aborted raid on Brunswick. It was later revealed that the crews' relief at seeing the three-lane Carnaby runway induced many to forego normal landing procedures and to approach the runway 'in droves'; others, electing to try their luck elsewhere but finding, too late, that the fog extended far inland, came to grief on the North Yorkshire Moors. Carnaby, however, possessed no debriefing or accommodation facilities, and several hours of waiting for any kind of transportation, either to nearby home bases or even into Bridlington to find a bed and breakfast, was often a wearying chore after a combat mission.

While the problems of dealing with multi-based personnel continued even up to the end of the war, the handling and return of the aircraft themselves, either back to their units or to 'write-off' centres, required a prodigious administration effort. To quote just one example, a 102 Squadron pilot, Hugh Tyson, reported seeing 'at least a hundred Halifaxes, Lancasters and Stirlings parked nose over tail in precise order, in the loop at the end of the runway and flowing back onto it, all awaiting clearance to fly back to their home stations'. But the weather remained unremittingly grim with ice, which, if left unattended, became an inch thick on the runway. The heroics performed in keeping Carnaby operational are accurately recorded in Geoffrey Williams's highly descriptive book *Flying Through Fire*. Published in 1995, it details the history of FIDO at all the UK locations and is well worth tracking down.

Carnaby was the setting for many dramatic wartime events which, although regarded as almost commonplace at the time, would make significant headlines today. One of these involved

Squadron Leader Tony Iveson DFC remembers well his landing at Carnaby with a 12,000lb 'Tallboy' bomb in his Lancaster's bomb bay.

a 617 Squadron pilot, Squadron Leader Tony Iveson, who experienced a technical problem while on a positioning flight from his base at Woodhall Spa in Lincolnshire to Lossiemouth in Scotland en route to attack the German battleship *Tirpitz*. Redirected to Carnaby, fortunately on a beautiful sunny afternoon, he made a tentative approach and touched down with a 12,000lb 'Tallboy' in his Lancaster's bomb bay. I would add that apart from being shot down over the English Channel in late 1940, Tony had become the only ex-fighter pilot to join the famed 'Dambuster' squadron; along with other bombing missions he participated in all three of the squadron's raids on the battleship, which culminated in it capsizing in Norway's Tromsø fjord on 12 November 1944. I mention this because while I was an aeroplane-mad youngster, forever dashing out of the house at the sound of any aero engine, Tony, some thirteen years my senior, was seriously engaged in attacking the enemy. However, jumping forward several decades to 1986, our paths crossed in professional circumstances and we have subsequently remained firm friends. Today, aged over 90, Tony has energetically spearheaded the drive to provide the memorial in London's Green Park to the 55,573 members of Bomber Command who lost their lives in the Second World War.

My wartime memories largely revolve around seeing groups of young men in blue uniforms with the white flashes in their forage caps indicating 'aircrew in training'. Many were engaged in shooting at clay pigeons fired over the town's boating pool for gunnery

RAF Lissett, now restored to farmland and hosting a twelve-unit wind turbine site, was once home to 158 Squadron. The sculpted metal memorial shown here was created by local artist Peter Naylor as a tribute to the 851 men of the squadron who lost their lives on active service. Unveiled on 16 May 2009, it cleverly depicts a seven-man crew walking towards you, whether viewed from the front or rear.

familiarisation, or sitting in the South Cliff Gardens just above the harbour, trying to cope with aircraft recognition charts. I wonder now what they made of cocky little devils like myself who constantly tried to impress them with our unerring ability to identify, from any angle, anything that flew, including Russian, Japanese and Italian types. I can recall our typical approach even to this day: 'Cor, don't you know that a Junkers 88 has its crew all at the front? A Blenheim's crew is all spaced out along the fuselage.' Just the kind of 'clever dick' remark I'm sure they wanted to hear from 10- and 11-year-old kids! The big difference was, of course, that these young gunners, many no more than 19 or 20 years old, struggling to take in the recognition features of, for example, a German night fighter, were all too aware that their lives and those of their crews were highly dependent on how well they had absorbed this specialist training. We, the self-proclaimed experts, simply went home to tea, smugly priding ourselves on how knowledgeable we thought we were.

Today, I permit myself an indulgent and recollective smile because my youngest grandson Giles, now aged 14, has told me he has become the Eastleigh Air Cadet Squadron's aircraft recognition instructor. Not only has he inherited the contagious disease of 'aircraft affiliation', for which I must shoulder some blame (there is no known cure), but both he and his elder brother Angus have become dedicated musicians and now form part of the Air Cadets' National Marching and Concert Bands, and I would be a very strange grandfather if I wasn't proud of that.

I sometimes cringe at the memory of those wartime sessions, and hope that the brave young men whose sacrifice is recorded in a poignant permanent testimonial at Lissett, home to 158 Squadron (which in an odd numerical quirk lost 851 aircrew), made all due allowances for our raw enthusiasm. To their eternal credit, they seemed very tolerant and on occasions – God bless 'em – even asked for our advice!

RAF personnel who serviced and crewed the three seaplane tenders of 1104 Marine Craft Unit, used for rescuing downed airmen and bombing range patrol, were much in evidence in the town. Service personnel stretched the town's entertainment facilities to the limit. Recreational use of The Spa was, I believe, limited due to its housing of some of the airmen

An Air Sea Rescue Launch of 1104 Marine Craft Unit leaves Bridlington harbour. (David Wright Collection)

under training. The Lounge, Regal and Winter Gardens cinemas, however, all located within the space of 100yd along the Promenade, were filled to capacity every night, with their respective queues almost overlapping along the pavement. The Regal Cinema was by far the 'poshest', and emitted a unique and sophisticated aroma that contributed to the feeling of having had a special night out. The Winter Gardens had a far more intimate atmosphere (in more ways than one) and was the most popular venue in town. It was managed by Mr Mundy, who, come rain or shine, appeared outside in black tie to either raise or depress the spirits of the crush waiting to get in. All too often his 'two single one and nines only' (8p in today's money) was not the offer many couples wanted to hear, but it did sometimes allow me to appear from way back in the line and plonk my money down while their deliberations were going on. With my immediate aim of getting inside accomplished, the next concern as one entered the temple of gloom, with the projector beam struggling to fight its way through the dense fog of cigarette smoke, was to hope the vacant seat so valiantly fought for wasn't behind a woman wearing a tall hat. With continuous performances running throughout the afternoons and evenings, it was common practice for many to stay put once admitted, especially if the film was, shall we say, of secondary importance.

Some of the kids had discovered that the emergency exit doors in the Winter Gardens gentlemen's toilets could be opened from the inside, thus allowing a lemming-like influx of non-paying young guests to enter and scuttle on to the front rows. This little scam didn't last long, however, before Mr Mundy solved the problem by locking the push bars on the emergency exits. This was not, perhaps, the wisest of solutions considering the possibility of an enemy raid and would undoubtedly have fallen foul of today's 'Ealth and Safety requirements (Gawd Help Us)! A rather sinister woman, wearing a Church Lads Brigade-style forage cap and dark glasses, would wave her torch along the front rows demanding to see tickets. Those offered up had no doubt been used for several previous performances. Those of us who were slightly more law-abiding would, just to be on the safe side, hold on to our damp entry paperwork until we emerged into daylight.

I should point out that Mr Mundy had a worthy competitor in Johnny Higo, who, with his dark, wavy, brilliantined hair and pencil-line moustache, performed a similar sartorial function at the Lounge Cinema. Through his working with my mother I knew him fairly well and we usually had a word or two as he cycled home for tea, prior to his black-tie appearance in the evening. His Valentino looks didn't seem so strange in those days, but they would certainly turn a few heads today. What with my mother on duty at the cash kiosk and Johnny at the queue control point, I could always gain entrance to the Lounge Cinema.

I recall the eager anticipation of a well-advertised wartime dive-bombing demonstration in Bridlington Bay by Fleet Air Arm aircraft. Presumably it would have involved either Blackburn Skuas or Fairey Barracudas, but bad weather caused it to be cancelled and we youthful enthusiasts had to settle for a static display by the RAF's recruiting team in the Floral Pavilion. At least I learned how to operate a practice-bomb release mechanism, but it was undoubtedly a wet and disappointing anticlimax. At age 10, growing up and joining the RAF seemed a long way off.

From 1942 the Avro Lancaster was the RAF's preferred deliverer of high explosives, but the Yorkshire airfields of Bomber Command's No 4 Group remained largely populated by the less revered Handley Page Halifax. It was an unfortunate and fatal fact that the early production versions of the Halifax exhibited a variety of problems that caused much concern at operational level. Not least of these was the infamous rudder stalling which, with two engines dead on one side, led to many crashes on final approach, especially at night. The Mk III version, with the removed nose turret, the installation of more powerful Bristol Hercules engines and a redesigned rectangular fin and rudder assembly, later proved to be an entirely different proposition.

I still remember the occasion in 1943, standing on a beach breakwater in front of The Spa Theatre with a fair amount of water under my feet, when a Halifax suddenly appeared at roof-top height from the town side. I happened to be looking out to sea at the time, so neither saw nor heard it, until this enormous black bundle of rivets in close formation passed very low and directly over me, causing a panic-driven jump into the waves and the involuntary intake of much salt water. I was not best pleased at the time since the pilot was probably some young buck showing off to an admiring girlfriend on the South Pier. Ah well, just in case it was a machine belonging to one of the Free French Halifax 346 *Guyenne* or 347 *Tunisie* Squadrons based a bit further down the road at Elvington, *C'est la guerre!*

A 78 Squadron Halifax II at Linton-on-Ouse sporting the triangular fin and rudder arrangement, the early nose turret and the Merlin engines, which together did not endear this variant to its crews. (*Halifax in Action*, Squadron/Signal Publications, 1984)

The advent of Bristol Hercules engines, a redesigned nose, and above all the introduction of the rectangular fins and rudders, transformed the Halifax into a first-class aircraft. (*Halifax in Action*)

You're now (almost) forgiven. I have long been aware of the story that a low-flying Halifax removed the flagpole above the central glass dome of The Spa ballroom. This escapade remains unconfirmed, but my 'ducking' experience that day leads me to think it was entirely probable. It might even have been the same flight, but I was too busy recovering from my sudden immersion to follow that particular mad bugger's progress!

The most unusual wartime memories I have are of the occasional appearances over the town by the P-38G Lightnings of the USAAF's 78th Fighter Group, based across the Humber at Goxhill in Lincolnshire, and the all-black Northrop P-61 Black Widow twin-boom night fighters, operating from Scorton in North Yorkshire. However, my strongest recollections are of the immense No 4 Group bomber force circling for height over Bridlington in the late evenings (with Double British Summer Time it never seemed to get dark), before heading east. The main point of departure was Flamborough Head, which not only provided a pivotal navigational feature for the RAF, but also formed a distinctive landmark for incoming German raiders attacking Yorkshire towns and villages. Later in the war, though certainly not comparable to the number of V-1 flying bombs which landed in southern England, Yorkshire's fields saw the unwelcome arrival of several air-launched vehicles, which fell well short of intended targets further inland.

The blue uniforms of the RAF were, by far, the most numerous in Bridlington, but those of the army were also much in evidence, especially in the weeks leading up to D-Day. The Stuart and Sherman tanks of the 1st Polish Armoured Regiment always impressed us lads as, with pennants fluttering from their radio masts and commanders sporting large binoculars leaning out of the turrets, they ground their noisy way round the town and out up Bessingby Hill into the Wolds countryside on daily manoeuvres. The tanks' tracks soon caused the town's roadside kerb edges to disintegrate, much to the chagrin of the older population. No consideration for the residents, was their cry; none whatsoever! We local boys, unhampered by such civic concerns, found it frustratingly difficult to hitch a ride in a Bren-gun carrier, which though plentiful were sensibly regarded by the crews as not worth the risk of injury. Other units belonging to the Green Howards and 17/21 Lancers were also billeted in the town prior to leaving for the southern embarkation ports. The amount

American twin-boom fighters were unusual visitors to the local area, so the sight of a P-61 Black Widow following the railway line from Bridlington to its likely base at Scorton in North Yorkshire caused me some excitement. (Paul Bright Collection)

Perhaps unwilling to risk penalty points on his licence, a Sherman tank driver of the 1st Polish Armoured Regiment observes the long arm of the law. No doubt Hitler's Panzer Divisions would have had to toe a similar line had the invasion taken place. (Bridlington Public Library)

of military activity on the roads and in the skies was intense, and how all this was ever co-ordinated into a coherent D-Day plan I still find absolutely amazing.

In the early days of the war there was a great deal of competition between one's schoolmates as to who could collect the most bomb shrapnel or, on the rare occasion, machine-gun bullets. I came across a number of these items one morning at the end of St John's Walk. Quite frequently the shrapnel was still hot, which required it to be buried out of sight before other schoolboy predators took possession. Sometimes the pieces were too big to fit in the large-necked jars provided by our mothers, but it went against the grain to miss out on the chance of a good swap with similar-minded colleagues.

On one occasion, my younger friend David Wright and I set off after Sunday School on a long trek into the countryside to try to find incendiary bomb fins, then considered by the youthful cognoscenti to be prized collectors' items. Unfortunately, this adventure became rather protracted, for our ramble took us well out of Bridlington to Boynton village, some 3 or 4 miles distant, and it was nearly bedtime by the time we wearily returned to find our parents gathered in the street, worried sick and about to inform the police we were missing. Being the oldest, I got my one and only thwack across the backside from my grandma. But what hurt the most was the fact that we hadn't found any bomb fins. Such ventures, however, could and occasionally did end in tragedy. German raiders were now reported to be including anti-personnel devices within the usual mix of incendiary and high-explosive

St George's secondary modern school, which I first attended in 1944, shared the cost of German bombing, losing its gymnasium and assembly hall, fortunately without loss of life. Priory Church in the background luckily escaped damage. (Bridlington Public Library)

bombs. Posters depicting these Butterfly Bombs – so called because the casing split into two halves as it descended, thus arming the fuse – were placed in prominent positions at the local schools. DO NOT TOUCH OR PICK UP was an unmistakeable warning that certainly made an impact on me. No one I knew ever came across one, but the odd lurid tale of someone who had paid the price of curiosity sometimes found its way into the school announcements. It was not until after the war that it was disclosed the attacks involving these nasty items were, strangely, limited to raids on RAF Wattisham, Cleethorpes and Grimsby in Lincolnshire. At the time, the government imposed a general news blackout on the effectiveness of this weapon in case the enemy increased its usage.

Later in the war, the aim was to show off the most varied collection of military insignia. With so many army units of different nationalities passing through the town, the rewards, if one was prepared to sweep out a billet or run an errand, were pretty good. One Belgian soldier allowed me to fire a service rifle from the upstairs window of a hotel billet in Queen Street straight across the harbour. I can imagine the furore and raised eyebrows such an event would now occasion in today's 'Ealth and Safety circles. I also had a marked advantage in having to pass on my way to secondary school, in 1945, the so-called Laundry Field Internment Camp, holding German prisoners of war. The British soldiers guarding the camp were virtually non-existent, no doubt well huddled down in some makeshift hut over a brew. This suited me just fine, for it was amazing what could be obtained through the wire fence for an open-ended packet of five small Woodbine cigarettes, kindly provided by my indulgent mother (still May at this stage). The badges I managed to acquire, some now judged to be extremely rare, have remained in my possession, although with three adolescent and enquiring grandsons now expressing an interest, I'm uncertain as to how much longer my collection can remain intact.

Unlike today, I was then a very slender youth and when word got around that coal – that rare and precious wartime commodity – had arrived at the local rail depot in the bitter winter of 1944, my mother was offered the loan of a heavy wooden barrow. It had small, cast-iron wheels and even when empty would have strained a donkey in pulling a much-awaited ration home. Hauling this contraption fully loaded required the strength of Hercules and when I came up against an icy kerb edge, my slender muscles simply couldn't manage it. Fortunately, other adults were on hand to get the barrow moving again. Once home, it proved impossible to manoeuvre the barrow down the narrow passage between the terraced houses, whereupon a final back-breaking effort was required to transfer the contents by hand shovel to the outhouse that contained the coal bunker and the external toilet. But compared to the wartime problems of other families, such trivial difficulties scarcely scratched the surface and life simply went on. It was the 'done' thing, for example, to cut newspapers into strips for use as toilet paper in the outside loo, or to take it down to the social epicentre of Bridlington (the local fish and chip shop) for wrapping the food in. Different paper, I hasten to add!

My boyhood fascination with warlike preparations was, given the circumstances, entirely normal and through new pals having older relatives in the Royal Observer Corps, I got the opportunity to see quality publications such as the *Air Training Corps Gazette*, *The Aeroplane Spotter*, the *Aircraft Recognition Journal*, *Flight* and *The Aeroplane* magazines. The contents of these I absorbed like a sponge, and having got it into my blood, this deep interest in aviation has remained with me throughout the years. I am told by similarly afflicted ancient colleagues that this may be due to being bitten by a rabid aeroplane when I wasn't looking!

I strongly recall standing up in an otherwise studious class and shouting, 'Look at that! Douglas Bostons!' as an aerial armada swept past the classroom window. My enthusiastic observation wasn't, however, appreciated by my teacher. All I can add is that the following

'All the latest Gen – Read all abaht it!' *The Aeroplane Spotter* was a difficult magazine to get hold of during the war. One needed friends with older relatives in the Royal Observer Corps to even stand a chance.

VOLUME 1 NUMBER 9

AIRCRAFT
RECOGNITION

THE INTER-SERVICES JOURNAL

MAY 1943

The monthly inter-services *Aircraft Recognition* journal was even rarer than *The Aeroplane Spotter*, although the odd copy did filter through. It wasn't until my later time in the RAF that I was able to place a large number into a good home. Mine!

day, despite being laid low with chicken pox, I was still fired up with a memory that has lingered to the present day. Further excitement ensued when, during an afternoon playtime, a large barrage balloon that had broken free from its moorings was seen to be heading directly towards the school. After being quickly ushered into the playground shelters, we waited silently as the silver monster's dangling ground attachment cable continued to knock slates and tiles off nearby buildings, including our school, before it was eventually shot down over Bridlington Bay.

To further emphasise my obsession with 'the air', in 1943 I made an unscripted yet impassioned appeal to the entire Oxford Street Junior School assembly to support a Wings for Victory Week. This featured a Hurricane fighter in the Cenotaph Gardens, along with a large thermometer-style graphic aid showing the amount of money raised from local contributions. Standing beside the fighter I was in awe of its size.

Whenever I visit Bridlington I always take a stroll down St John's Walk and, rolling back the years, relive some of those boyhood memories. Pleasant though they are, I am saddened nowadays to see the state of neglect that has overtaken No 9. Time has not been kind to my old home, yet all the surrounding properties have, more than half a century on, remained well kept and little changed. Perhaps I expect too much!

2

YOUTHFUL PURSUITS

My wartime keenness to raise national morale, though no doubt commendable, was soon eclipsed by visits to the town firstly by (then) General Sir Bernard Montgomery on 8 February 1944, followed by King George VI on 22 March, accompanied by the queen and Princess Elizabeth, who was undertaking her first public engagement. I managed to secure a prime vantage point for Montgomery's arrival by standing on the town hall wall directly opposite the railway station exit. After his car had departed, I scooted alongside the Gypsy Race river (which we always called Beckside) just in time to see him enter the drive leading up to the Bridlington Grammar School for Boys. Then, excitement over, it was but a couple of hundred yards round the corner to home and lunch.

As with the local exhortations to raise money for the Wings for Victory campaign, similar efforts took place to involve the public with the Salute the Soldier and HMS *Bridlington* corvette cash-raising ventures. I'm sure that these propagandist appeals to Bridlington's population were well heeded, as were other events throughout the country, but the local outcry against the tank tracks ruining the pavement edges makes me wonder just how strong the support was in certain quarters.

My school reports at this time showed a good average ability in all subjects, but when it came to sitting for the all-important scholarship for entry to the local grammar school in 1944, I failed to make the grade. I still can't figure out why I wasn't successful, but missing this once-only chance to gain a quality education causes me much regret. However, as my grandmother always impressed upon me, 'As one door closes, another opens', and when faced with a secondary modern education more orientated towards the manual trades, I resolved to roll up my sleeves and get on with it. Unimpeded by today's Health and Safety restrictions, my last year or two of formal schooling, just after the war ended, saw me take on a variety of errand-boy delivery jobs in the evenings and at weekends. I recall, on one occasion, my overloaded greengrocery delivery bike falling over and depositing three customers' worth of contents into the path of busy traffic along Quay Road. Mr Jefferson, the shop owner, was not overly sympathetic, for while picking up the stray carrots and potatoes between oncoming cars, he told me I was fired. But the most taxing of these after-school activities was as Mrs Gravill's butcher shop delivery boy in the harsh snowbound winter of 1946/47. With the snow piled several feet high on both sides of the road in that exceptional winter, I pushed my bike (riding was impossible) with its big wickerwork basket around the town. I can now imagine that this exercise inspired the iconic Hovis bread advertisement, which showed a

King George VI, Princess Elizabeth and Queen Elizabeth visiting Bridlington on 22 March 1944. (David Money Collection)

young boy pushing his way to the top of Shaftesbury's Gold Hill, just a mile or so away from where I presently live. But my experience was, I think, even more demanding than his. It took hours to deliver – on an enamelled metal tray – what rationed meat I could separate from the melted mush that had started out as clear-cut orders for the Old Town, Queensgate and Hilderthorpe areas. Though the customers' names were pencilled in on pristine sheets of greaseproof paper, those on the orders at the bottom of the basket were soon unreadable and all too often I had to rely on 'by guess and by God' to help me out. Though never averse to nibbling a bit off the suet surrounding a kidney, squeezing a bit of filling from a sausage or easing the corner from a slice of corned beef to offset my boyish hunger pangs, I don't recall anyone complaining about being short-changed. My customers were always very friendly and understanding, their attitude no doubt a carryover from the old wartime 'press on' spirit. Their threepenny-bit tips were also much appreciated, as I was then saving up for a new Raleigh Robin Hood bike from J.R. Taylor's Cycle and Pram Emporium.

This particular winter has long been regarded as the snowiest, though not the coldest, since official record-keeping began. Some measure of the difficulties experienced in trying to clear the main transportation routes can be gained from the fact that Rolls-Royce Derwent centrifugal compressor jet engines, a distinct rarity at the time, mounted on trolleys, were used on a number of railway lines in the north. However, despite creating much noise and

Right: Jet engine power was used to clear certain sections of railway lines in North Yorkshire during the exceptionally snowbound winter of 1946/47.

Below: They look harmless enough. Mrs Gray – Akela – was the Baptist Church Wolf Cub Pack leader. Standing just behind her right shoulder, I for one found her sufficiently attractive to offset any thoughts of deserting.

apparent snow movement, they met with only limited success. Indeed, the hard-packed snow presented such resistance that the engines, though generating 2,000lb of thrust, were forced backwards. Not quite what the inventor, Sir Frank Whittle, had had in mind when he was far-sightedly seeing the way forward for aircraft propulsion. I would refer the reader to a highly descriptive book, *Frozen in Time*, by Ian McCaskill and Paul Hudson for chilling reminders of that difficult winter.

Coincident with my various errand-boy duties, I became a Senior Sixer in the 5th Bridlington Baptist Church Wolf Cub pack. Here, the main attraction was undoubtedly the scoutmaster's pretty wife, Mrs Gray, who as Akela ran the Cubs. Little did she know how I felt about her. Well, maybe she did, but 'Dib, dib, dob, keep your mind on the job' wasn't too easy when she was around. Along with my other young buddies I was fast growing up, and at times, with no father around to explain the mysteries of life, this tended to make things rather difficult. My newfound masculine awareness was, without question, due to the combined effects of youthful hormonal changes, Bridlington's invigorating sea air and in no small measure the unattainable and attractive Mrs Gray.

My efforts to acquire proficiency badges met with only limited success. One attempt to gain an aeromodeller's badge saw me purchase a Skyleader balsa wood kit for an obscure American biplane. Not having anyone around with any constructional skills to draw on, I soldiered on, attaching in crude fashion the upper wing to the fuselage with pins from grandma's sewing box. The whole thing was a terrible mess, especially after I coated it with a light-blue gloss paint I found in a rusty tin in the outside coalhouse. Nevertheless, hoping for some points for initiative and effort, I put it into a shoebox and set off to show the scout district commissioner. No one was at home when I arrived and as it was pouring with rain, I put a hastily written note inside the package and left it on the doorstep. Maybe he considered the whole thing to be a joke in doubtful taste, but as I've not yet had any kind of reply, I think my chances of gaining recognition as a budding aeromodeller are fast beginning to fade. It was the same with knot tying. All I ever achieved was a sense of desperation when my sheepshank, or whatever it was, came unravelled at the slightest pull. And yet, by some miracle, I became the Senior Sixer, which doesn't say a great deal for the creative abilities of the rest of the pack.

We hoped it wasn't aiming at us! The Fairey Barracuda, though effective as a naval dive-bomber, wasn't the most aesthetically pleasing of designs. The Fairey-Youngman flaps and other external excrescences earned it the title the Fairey 'flying Christmas tree'.

I also have an abiding memory of a particularly wet and miserable week's cub camp under canvas at South Cave near Brough. Not having Bear Grylls' outlook on life, this proved to be not my scene at all, but it was almost worth it to see Fairey Barracudas being built at the Blackburn factory close by, carrying out dive-bombing practice on a nearby range.

No sexual distractions were present when, instead of becoming a Scout, I elected to join the Christ Church Lads Brigade (CLB) under the strict but friendly command of a First World War veteran, Captain Chalkley. His order of 'Eyes front, right dress! Do get it together!', followed by a general inspection by his lieutenant, Ian Gilmour, certainly got us scurrying about. Recalling our disparate ages and sizes, comedian Terry-Thomas's popular catchphrase, 'What a shower', might well have been coined to describe our weekly marches around the town. Though hardly on a par with the Hitler Youth for regimentation, discipline or motivation, the CLB did provide a mild insight into what uniformed life and team effort might hold in store.

At about this time it was suggested by my headmaster that I should leave school and start a 'proper' job in the local National Westminster Bank, but I declined this offer to become an office boy in Pinkney's Estate Agency. By coincidence, this was located in the same street where, some fourteen years earlier, my mother had worked in the footwear store. My duties quickly boiled down to lighting the coal fires in the office, riding my bike around the town to collect rents and doing odd jobs at Field House, where Mr Pinkney himself lived – and all for the princely sum of five shillings (25p) a week. One of the tenants I collected rent from was Mrs May Holbrook at No 30 Watsons Avenue. On one occasion I could hardly help but notice her freckle-faced daughter peering over her shoulder, no doubt curious to see who this young, golden-haired Adonis could be (I could add tall, broad-shouldered and extremely handsome but, well, modesty forbids). Little did I realise that I was getting a first glimpse of

Bridlington's Christ Church on Quay Road. This picture, taken around the turn of the nineteenth century, shows the home of the Church Lads Brigade (CLB) some forty years later. Little had changed. (David Neave)

Why should England tremble? We may not be in step, but at least we were marching in the same direction. I am in the second line of the CLB, nearest the camera.

Thelma, my future wife. Though for many years I would innocently admit to having been a 'rent boy', this is a description I would avoid like the plague today. Rent *collector* maybe, for one cannot be too careful in these changing times.

One thing that didn't change throughout the war was our radio, which continued to work despite the 'atmospherics' and the occasional failure of valves which were difficult to replace. Soon after D-Day, however, and after being alerted by other lads to the slick presentations put out by the American Forces Network, I soon became an ardent swing band fan, with Glenn Miller's American Band of the Allied Expeditionary Force topping the list. His unique orchestrations meant that British bands, still locked into pre-war-style arrangements, simply couldn't compete. The loss of this hugely charismatic band leader over the Channel, just before Christmas 1944, was an enormous blow to the Allied and even German troops, although his band continued to give concerts in France, Holland and Germany until returning to America in August 1945.

Without wanting to dwell too long on the Nazi theme, I remember well the arrival in Bridlington, just after the war, of a Mercedes 540K Special Roadster sports car, said to have been owned by Reichsmarschall Hermann Goering. Painted in 'aviation blue', Goering's favourite colour, and called the Blue Goose, this magnificent machine was parked for a short period outside Notarriani's ice-cream parlour in Prince Street. We youngsters were allowed a quick running-board inspection before it continued on its nationwide tour. It occurred to me later that although the car was constructed with bullet-proof glass and was specially reinforced to withstand running over an unfriendly landmine, it still lacked any kind of roof protection. Where was the sense in that? No wonder the Germans lost the war.

Thelma, plus freckles, in 1947; not
exactly love at first sight, but not far off.

Goering's Mercedes 540K Special
Roadster paid a visit to Bridlington during
a post-war tour of Britain.

Let's talk about cricket, a subject I can hold forth on for as long as anyone might be
prepared to listen. This, I've noticed, isn't usually very long if I slip into Victor Meldrew
mode, which I'm told I invariably do. I can barely encompass the changes that have taken
place over the past sixty years, but I rest somewhat assured by the fact that few of my
ancient contemporaries can either.

At one time the County Championship was a straightforward affair, with each side playing each other twice. The addition of various festival games, and the icing on the cake provided by a Test series with the visiting touring side, was an additional bonus that was much looked forward to. What could be simpler? Such was the cricket world I was familiar with when, with a sandwich pack and young companion, David Williams, in my tender care, I first attended the Scarborough Cricket Festival at North Marine Road in 1947. Yorkshire versus the MCC was, by tradition, the season's opening fixture and under blue skies I was already anticipating a foregone Yorkshire victory – a little prematurely as it turned out, as the pre-war England and Warwickshire captain, R.E.S. Wyatt, resisted the county bowling to score a dour and most unwelcome 141. A.B. Sellers, that cast-iron leader of the late 1930s Yorkshire side, led the team out after the tea interval and I remember his purposeful look over the shoulder at the pavilion clock, probably envisaging his first pint of the evening. The match, however, went the full three-day distance and despite a Len Hutton century in the second innings, the MCC pulled off a win by 59 runs. In my book, that wasn't supposed to happen.

Perhaps of more esoteric value, as I leaned over the pavilion rails towards two old chaps wrapped in coats and rugs to keep warm, were the autographs of Yorkshire stalwart John Tunnicliffe, who played 472 games for the county and was *Wisden*'s Cricketer of the Year

Bridlington Trinity United fielded a very strong and successful junior team in the late forties. Though called upon to make a modest goalkeeping contribution, I might, after sixty years, concede that the goal-hungry forwards were the architects of success.

Another Job by East Lancashire Coach Builders (Bridlington) Ltd.
Bessingby Way, Bridlington. *This blotter belongs to L. Cuddas' drawing office.*

BUILDERS OF
DOUBLE & SINGLE
DECK BODIES
FOR TROLLEY,
PETROL and OIL
VEHICLES OF
COMPOSITE and
ALL-METAL
CONSTRUCTION

FOR
FURTHER
DETAILS
SPECIFICATIONS
ETC.
" Please write "

A Double Deck Trolley Bus Body of composite construction
on Sunbeam Chassis. For Tees-side Rail-less Traction Board.

This East Lancashire Coach Building Company advertising blotter, *c.* 1949, is the only tangible reminder I have of my first practical working days.

for 1901, and H.D.G. Leveson-Gower, an old ex-Surrey and England player who was the main co-ordinator of festival fixtures in the post-war period. My first sighting of professional cricket was all rather awe-inspiring, following the fragmented radio commentaries relaying MCC's winter of humiliation in Australia (not the first, or last), wherein we lost the 1946–47 Test series 3-0.

By 1948 I was seriously into playing football and cricket, and it irked me considerably to think that while almost all of my sporting mates were apprentices of one kind or another, there I was messing about in a clerical non-job. Also influencing my outlook was a deep admiration for Bert Smith, who lived just a few doors away in St John's Walk. Bert, my senior by a few years, and a local amateur lightweight boxer, later moved on to the professional circuit, winning most of his contests before spending some sixty years within the sport's national administration. Meeting annually as we still do, I think Bert, now in his eighties and still very fit, would provide a boxing challenge for anyone!

Within a few short months I abandoned the estate agency business and with just days to spare before the entry cut-off date of my fifteenth birthday, I became a works apprentice at the East Lancashire Coach Building Company on the newly constructed Bessingby Industrial Estate. Here, my first job was to assist Stan Hill, an ex-Pioneer Corps veteran who was single-handedly building a large timber storage shed. Never in my long experience have I worked alongside someone so incapable of forming the simplest sentence without including an obscenity. However, he once remarked: 'Always make a show, lad.' I took this to mean that when faced with several tasks of varying complexity, you should do the easy ones first and leave the harder ones until the end. Then, when the boss comes round, he can see that you have at least been busy doing something; alternatively, a lot of head-scratching trying to solve a problem with nothing to show for it doesn't impress anyone. Probably the wisest words Stan ever uttered, and ones I have never forgotten.

Things were indeed looking up. Not only was I now in a working environment that I enjoyed, but I was acquiring practical skills that were to serve me well throughout my life. In addition, career ambition was beginning to make itself felt. This clearly would entail a long climb to overcome my earlier educational shortcomings. Day and night school subjects, such as mathematics and technical drawing, soon progressed from the City and Guilds level attained at Scarborough Technical College to a National Certificate (Mechanical Engineering) at Hull Technical College. I was also greatly encouraged by a year-long spell in the company's drawing office, working alongside a young man, Alan Miles, who to this day I regard as one of the finest draughtsmen I ever worked with. In those days, final drawings were produced using Indian ink on waxed linen sheets, any mistakes having to be rectified by scratching out the offending lines with an old-fashioned razor blade. This tedious procedure naturally bred a careful attitude towards accurate penmanship and getting things right first time, thereby reinforcing the maxim already taught in the works as the 'measure twice and cut once' technique. Today, it is still anathema to see a line of screws with slots out of line, a less-than-perfect painted edge on windows and doors or, in the garden, a carelessly cut edge to a flower bed border. Maintaining my insistence on a 'perfect curve' for edges in the garden usually causes my wife to raise her eyebrows in resignation, until I remind her that it was her perfect curves that attracted me to her in the first place. (No answer to that one, chaps.) Nevertheless, determined to have the last word, she accuses me of having a local corporation gardener's outlook and tells me to 'get a life'. She may well have a point but I'm too advanced in years to change now.

In recalling those early days at East Lancashire's factory, one event springs to mind that was to become one of the most memorable in my life. For any reader not disposed towards cricket I suggest skipping the next few pages, for now follows a classic case of the cricket bore's 'I was there'. It started with a Boddy's coach trip to the Headingley cricket ground in Leeds on 24 July 1948; we were going to watch the third day of the Fourth Test between England, captained by Norman Yardley, and Australia, led by Don Bradman. Setting off from 'Brid' at 6.30 a.m. on a wet Saturday morning, my heart sank, for as the journey progressed, so did the intensity of the rain. To observe one's heroes in the flesh was a rare and unbelievably exciting prospect, for the only other opportunity was on a frustratingly short, twenty-second clip on a Pathé newsreel at the local cinema. This would always show the pitch, invariably shortened to appear about 2yd long, the captains tossing the coin and cheering spectators or a player retrieving the ball from the boundary. Never was there much in the way of batting or bowling action.

Though not pessimistic by nature, I was convinced there would be no play as we approached Leeds. The size of the crowd snaking round the ground further depressed my spirits, but wonder of wonders, after we tagged on to the back of the enormous queue, it moved steadily forward until, to my tremendous relief, we finally entered the ground. The weather miraculously cleared by the start of play and I was truly beside myself with excitement when Hassett and Bradman walked down the pavilion steps in bright sunshine to face England's pacemen, Alec Bedser and Dick Pollard. Bradman had built up a tremendous reputation for achieving runs at Leeds, his pre-war Test appearances having produced 334 in 1930, 304 in 1934 and 103 in 1938. So, the inevitable question on everybody's lips was, would The Don flay the English attack yet again?

He had made 31 not out on the previous evening, so was no doubt warming to the task when play began, before a delivery from Bedser struck him a painful blow on the thigh and laid him low. It was shortly after this, and with only eight minutes gone into the morning session that, with his score at 33, a fine delivery from Pollard uprooted his off stump. After a moment's gasp from the capacity crowd, a roar erupted; such noise, it is said, has never been exceeded on any cricket ground. But the crowd's elation at having snared Australia's legendary run-maker was immediately tempered by the realisation that Bradman was *not* going to entertain us that day. Mixed feelings indeed! My hero did go on to score a century in Australia's second innings of 404, which at the time was the highest fourth innings recorded to win a Test match, but although this kept his century-making record at Headingley intact, it afforded me small consolation. Having read many books extolling Bradman's batting prowess, the one opportunity I had to witness his magic had been compressed into a spell that lasted less than ten minutes and which produced only two runs. I never really forgave Pollard for that dismissal any more than I gave Warwickshire spin bowler Eric Hollies credit for bowling Bradman, second ball for nought, in his next and final Test appearance at the Oval, thus leaving the great man with a career Test average of 99.94. A single four would have ensured the magical 100.00, but the gods said 'no' and confirmed in my mind that life isn't always fair.

What I found to be most distasteful, however, was that following Bradman's dismissal, such was the jealousy of two famed pre-war Australian teammates – Jack Fingleton and Bill O'Reilly, then covering the 1948 tour as journalists – that they laughed with undisguised glee, knowing that The Don's imminent retirement would not give him another opportunity to reach the coveted figure. I thought Fingleton to be an excellent commentator and I do sincerely hope that I will eventually find something of substance that will prove this story to

First blow to England: Bradman is felled by a painful delivery from Alec Bedser. (*Yorkshire Evening Post*)

be untrue. Around fifty years later, in response to my professional enquiry as Cobham plc's archivist of whether Don and Sir Alan Cobham – Britain's leading pre-war pioneering flyer – had ever met, I received a personally typed aerogram from Sir Donald, as he had by then become, starting 'Dear Colin' and ending with his cherished autograph.

To partly offset the disappointment of not seeing a substantial innings from Bradman, I did see Neil Harvey, aged just 19, score his maiden Test century, along with sparkling fifties from Australia's Keith Miller, Ray Lindwall and a particularly aggressive 93 from Sam Loxton. As with my brief glimpse of the incomparable Bradman, I had an equally short sight of Ray Lindwall hurling down his thunderbolts at Scarborough. To my dismay, an all-too-familiar coastal mist rolled in causing play to be abandoned, but not before he had scattered the stumps of my other co-hero, Yorkshire's own Len Hutton, for a duck. What is it about cricket that can be so damned frustrating?

The three years between 1948 and 1951 were for me very eventful and no doubt character-forming, for during this period I played for Bridlington's first eleven teams at both football (Trinity United) and cricket, though not, I should add, as frequently or successfully as I would have liked. Nevertheless, this early 'blooding' introduced a competitive attitude towards life that has stood me in good stead.

```
                                    2 Holden Street,
                                    Kensington Park.
                                    S.A.  5068.
                                         14-10-96.

Dear Colin,
              This morning I received in the mail your
kind letter and the book.      Thankyou so much.
         In reply to your specific question the answer is NO
I did not have the pleasure of meeting Sir Alan.
         However as a small school boy I have vivid memories
of Ross & Keith Smith flying to Australia and their
route took them directly over the school I was attending
at Bowral - where the Bradman Museum now exists.
       . Also when I was in England in, I believe, 1930,
I had the pleasure of taking tea with Amy Johnson.
         So I've had some remote connection with flying.
         I look forward very much to reading the book
and hopefully my wife will also.     Sadly she is very
seriously ill with advanced cancer and getting treatment
every day.     This may take her mind off it for a while.

                    Again many thanks.

                    Sincerely,

                    Don Bradman
```

Above: Left-hander Neil Harvey on his way to a maiden Test century at Headingley in 1948. (*Yorkshire Evening Post*)

Left: Don Bradman could do little wrong (except get out) in my eyes. My deepest regret was that he was playing for Australia and not England. My respect for him was (if possible) further enhanced when I received his personal reply to a query made regarding a book I was researching on Sir Alan Cobham.

This publicity poster, *c.* 1949, though showing a highly idealistic impression of Bridlington's attractions, still conveys its gem-like setting on Yorkshire's east coast. (David Neave)

After much financial deliberation, I decided one day in 1948 to invest seven shillings and sixpence (37p) on my first flight. This was in a two-seat Auster based at Speeton and involved flying out over Flamborough Head, executing a tight circuit over Bridlington before making a straight run back to the airfield. Though obviously excited to be in the air, I found it a disorientating experience and difficult to distinguish familiar landmarks. The pilot, whose name I never learned, wasn't a great help, hardly saying a word during the fifteen-minute flight, and his battered trilby hat and pipe, which he retained upside down in his mouth, didn't create a particularly Biggles-like impression. I had however flown and unknowingly passed a small milestone on the road to an aviation career.

Perhaps today, the transition from eager childhood to that of uncertain young adulthood happens sooner than in my youth. I recall, however, that on reaching the age of 16 in 1949, relatively simple events began to take on a new and deeper significance. For example, it was exciting when the town, after slumbering through the winter, became alive with the influx of visitors. Crowds packed the North Pier on Whitsuntide Saturday, all straining to see the first smudge of smoke on the horizon as Bridlington's favourite pleasure steamer, the *Yorkshireman*, appeared from Hull, heading for the harbour. It also seemed particularly daring when, on returning from an away match, the cricket team bus stopped at the Black Swan pub in Brandesburton village so that older members of the team could bring half pints of strong cider or shandy outside for the young lads' eager and illicit delectation. But riding above all in my new awakening was the fact that I had fallen very much in love for the first time – well, the second time if one includes Mrs Gray – and my personal priorities now underwent a vigorous reshuffle. As already mentioned, career and social opportunities in Bridlington were conditioned by one's family background and I soon realised that I didn't have a great deal to offer. The girl's parents were of similar mind and, considering they owned a guesthouse on the posh side of town and were members of the local golf club, made it clear they didn't see me as either a long- or even

The *Yorkshireman* pleasure steamer plied its trade in Bridlington between 1928 and 1956 (excluding the war years). It was the main sailing attraction among others that included the *Royal Sovereign*, which was sunk during a wartime attack. *Yorkshireman's* arrival was always a keenly awaited arrival on the town's calendar. (Bridlington Public Library)

short-term suitor for their daughter. At the time, however, we both thought that young love would overcome parental objections. Accordingly, we attended the dances held at The Spa Royal Hall which was, and still is, the most desirable venue on the east coast; it frequently featured such great bands as those of Ted Heath, Joe Loss, Eric Winstone, Cyril Stapleton, Harry Roy, Harry Gold and his Pieces of Eight, Victor Sylvester and many more. Such easy access to this top-level entertainment, along with the excellent music provided by the stalwart local band leaders Ceres and Edwin Harper, was something we all took for granted. But my circumstances were about to change dramatically after my mother spotted a Fairey Aviation Company advertisement in the *Yorkshire Evening Post* calling for 'Design and detail draughtsmen. Training provided.'

East Lancashire's work in the late 1940s had largely consisted of taking in fleets of war-weary buses from various municipalities in the north, stripping them down to the chassis and rebuilding the coachwork. For about four years this had provided a steady flow of work but when it began to dry up, orders were taken for school furniture. This didn't excite me at all. I was certainly ready to flex my wings and my immediate reaction to the Fairey advertisement was, 'Yes, I'll go for it'. However, in my youthful exuberance, I gave little thought to either the separation from my girlfriend (naively thinking that we would cope with the break) or, more importantly, to the impact on my mother. Although the loss of even my meagre apprentice income would make her ability to pay the bills more precarious, she was, to her eternal credit, willing to push me out into the big wide world.

Above: The Spa Theatre and Opera House and The Spa Royal Hall, resurrected after a disastrous fire in 1932, has certainly had a chequered history. A meeting place for countless romantic encounters, including mine, it now offers an entertainment and conference complex second to none. (East Riding of Yorkshire County Council)

Right: Though often overtaken by the glamour of the 'big bands', it was Ceres and Edwin Harper who provided the staple weekly dancing attractions at The Spa during the late 1940s and early 1950s. (East Riding of Yorkshire County Council)

SPA ROYAL HALL
BRIDLINGTON
Manager for the Corporation, - H. J. POINTER

SUMMER SEASON - 1950

Commencing
WHIT-SATURDAY
MAY 27th

CERES HARPER
AND HIS
ORCHESTRA

with

AL DEANE
Canadian Tenor

Thanks for the mem..or...y

WEEKLY PROGRAMME

Except JUNE 19th to 24th (Bridlington Dance Festival.)

Monday - - MERRY GO ROUND. A Feast of Fun.
Tuesday - - OLD TIME DANCE.
Wednesday - FLOOR SHOW NIGHT. Concert, Cabaret, Dancing.
Thursday - MODERN DANCE. " **YORKSHIRE EVENING POST** " Dance Competition.
Friday - - CONCERT AND HIDDEN TALENT CONTEST.
Saturday - WEEK-END HOLIDAY DANCE.
Sunday - - SPECIAL CONCERT.

Sun Lounge - Cafe Restaurant - Palm Court - Bar
" Where Friends meet Friends "

(Above Programme subject to alteration without notice)
ALL SEATS BOOKABLE IN ADVANCE ON APPLICATION TO THE
ENTERTAINMENTS MANAGER, SPA ROYAL HALL

CUSTOMERS' VEHICLES ARE BROUGHT ON TO OUR PREMISES, DRIVEN BY OUR STAFF AND STORED AT CUSTOMERS' OWN RISK AGAINST DAMAGE HOWSOEVER CAUSED.

WE ACCEPT NO RESPONSIBILITY FOR GLASS AFTER VEHICLES FITTED WITH SAME HAVE LEFT OUR PREMISES.

EAST LANCASHIRE COACH BUILDERS
(BRIDLINGTON) LIMITED.

BUILDERS OF DOUBLE AND SINGLE DECK BODIES FOR TROLLEY, PETROL, AND OIL VEHICLES OF COMPOSITE AND METAL CONSTRUCTION.

LIGHT INDUSTRIAL ESTATE,
BESSINGBY WAY,
BRIDLINGTON.
E. YORKSHIRE.

OUR REF.:

TELEPHONE/GRAMS 4464/5.

To whom it may concern.

Colin Cruddas has been employed by this Company for three years since he was fifteen years of age. During this period he has been apprenticed to the vehicle building trade. For one year he has been receiving training in the Drawing Office.

Throughout his service with this Company he has shown himself to be keenly interested in the work, and he has been most industrious. He has had further educational training at Hull Technical College and holds the City and Guilds Certificate for Commercial Body Building. At the present time he is studying for the National Certificate for Engineering.

He is the type of young man who will make good progress in life because he is so conscientious in his work, pleasing in appearance, courteous and respectful to his superiors but still able to be very companionable to his fellow men in the shop. This is an adjunct in any young man.

I strongly recommend his for training as a draughtsman and feel sure that he will do well.

L.M.Garwood,M.B.E.,A.I.A.C.,
Managing Director & Secrtary.

I must have been doing something right!

Such were the ingredients that led to my new career. The Fairey Company invited me down to Hayes in Middlesex for an interview, to which I took a glowing letter of recommendation from East Lancashire's managing director, Major Garwood, and subsequently offered me a place in the drawing office school as a student apprentice. At that time the company had a strong reputation as a prime producer of naval aircraft. But so did its rival, Blackburn Aircraft Ltd, at Brough in East Yorkshire, which was much nearer to home. The difference was, however, that Fairey was prepared to offer a structured training, whereas Blackburn was not. Additionally, working in the London area was an exciting prospect and one I looked forward to with great anticipation.

The company's founder, Sir Richard Fairey, was a tall (6ft 7in), physically imposing individual who belonged to an elite band of aeronautical entrepreneurs. This included men such as Frederick Handley Page, Geoffrey de Havilland and Thomas Sopwith, who, mainly possessing an engineering background, had the good fortune when war broke out in 1914 to be well placed to undertake aircraft design and manufacture. Their commanding presence almost demanded everyone sat to attention whenever they passed through the office.

Not all of the Fairey designs proved successful; few, if any, of the aircraft companies could claim otherwise. However, in not only making the airframes but also the large sub-assemblies, such as undercarriages and propellers usually supplied by other specialist firms, Fairey ranked with the best and I felt proud to be joining the company. And so, within a few hundred yards of leaving the station, the train taking me south rolled past the East Lancashire Coach Building Company's twin blister-shaped buildings. Being an early Saturday morning there was no one in sight to wave to; had it been a weekday there might have been a few. But no matter; 'onwards and upwards' was the order of the day, and there was no going back now. The big adventure had begun.

3

FAIREY TALES

y eventual arrival at the North Hyde Road factory later that day proved less than auspicious. Having struggled with a heavy suitcase that seemed to weigh more than I did from the Hayes railway station up to the company's main gate security office, I found myself facing what could have passed for the deck of the *Mary Celeste*. There was no one anywhere to be seen. To my relief, Sergeant Vic Pepper (not to my knowledge associated with the Lonely Hearts Club Band) – clearly disturbed from a radio football commentary – finally appeared, vaguely irritated, from a back room in the security hut. 'Could you please direct me to the Fairey hostel,' I asked. No doubt wondering where this simpleton could possibly have come from, he explained that Fairey didn't have such an amenity. What had given me that idea? With suddenly no idea where I was going to stay that night, and with dusk fast descending, mild panic set in, but the redoubtable sergeant telephoned his mother-in-law, Mrs Came, in Hunters Grove, who kindly agreed to take me in for one week. One wonders how in all the previous correspondence the provision of temporary accommodation could have been overlooked by the company's personnel department. Even my mother had not deemed it necessary to question where I was going to stay, naturally assuming that in such a big firm, this kind of detail would be sorted out as a matter of course. But these things happen, or in this case didn't happen. As that dismal March afternoon eventually came to an end, and I found myself for the first time distanced from everything familiar, I was overcome with instant homesickness; and I must admit not a few tears fell on the pages of the letters I penned home to say that I had arrived safely and everything was fine.

When she called me downstairs for tea, Mrs Came suggested I might 'meet somebody' if I went along to the dance that evening at Fairey's works canteen. I did go along, but didn't meet anybody; instead I got seriously lost on the way home. In comparing the starkness of the canteen surroundings to the sumptuousness of Bridlington's Spa ballroom, along with thoughts of my girlfriend, I felt my morale and taste for adventure fast slipping away. Monday took an eternity to arrive, but when it did, I found my sense of excitement re-emerging and I duly set off to report for duty.

Entering the enormous drawing office, I could hardly believe the number of draughtsmen studiously engaged over their drawing boards. The office, too, emitted a most distinctive aroma, in its way every bit as unique as that given off within Bridlington's Regal Cinema or the strong-smelling cooling liquid which I later found characterised the machine shops.

Fairey's main administration block and wind tunnel building facing on to Hayes' North Hyde Road, looking much the same as on my arrival in 1951. Sergeant Pepper was housed in the first building on the left. (Fairey Archive)

Feeling nervous within my new surroundings, I was escorted to the office of the chief draughtsman, Ernie Norris. When he finally breezed in, hand outstretched, his greeting of 'Mornin' Bill' was certainly friendly enough, but someone had to explain that Ernie could never remember anybody's name and that a large number of the design staff jokingly referred to each other as 'Bill'. Being fair game as the latest newcomer, if I asked someone for information, the usual reply was 'Ask Bill, he knows more about it', leaving me without a clue as to who was being referred to.

After completing the formalities, Ernie told me that due to an administration error, it was too late for me to catch up on the drawing office course already in progress and I was going to have to wait for the start of the next one several months away. Coming on top of the personnel department's failure to advise me on accommodation matters, I began to wonder if moving south had been such a good idea. Ernie went on to say that during the waiting period I would work in the lofting section. My immediate reaction was that I didn't much care whether I worked upstairs in the loft or downstairs in the basement, but it was then explained that 'lofting' was a term inherited from the shipbuilding industry wherein information was transferred from drawings on to steel plates using chalk. CHALK! What had I done? My instant dismay was fortunately soon eased when it was made clear that the more refined technique used within the aircraft industry allowed data produced on the drawing board to be transferred on to specially sensitised aluminium sheets, 6ft by 4ft

Part of the design office. There were almost as many drawing boards behind the camera as there were in front. (Fairey Archive)

in size. This process required a small group of loftsmen, armed with brass pencils, spline curves and weights, often working on hands and knees to develop accurately at full scale the lightening holes, flanges and contours of wing ribs and fuselage frames as flat plate machining templates for production use.

My mentor was an affable chap called Charlie Francis who, in addition to his normal duties, spent a considerable time 'lofting' chassis for 9in-screen television sets which, routed out and bent into shape by a mate in the experimental shop next door, fitted neatly into his bicycle carrier bag. He then attached the necessary components at home and sold these simple working sets to his neighbours. I asked him one day why, if he was so interested in TV, he didn't go and work for the giant electronics firm EMI just across the railway tracks; he replied that if he had to do it for a living, the fun would go out of it. With television broadcasting just getting under way, and the opportunity to make some extra cash in the back pocket, I could see the temptation facing him, but I doubt that Fairey's management would have seen his pastime in quite the same light.

It was Charlie who introduced me to, as he described it, the 'Holy of Holies'. This was the partitioned-off area in the experimental department which, run by the highly

Chief draughtsman
Ernie Norris, first left
on the front row,
solved the problem
of recalling names by
calling everybody 'Bill'.
(Fairey Archive)

uncompromising Ernie Hutton, contained the mainly plywood mock-up of the company's
new Type Q or GR 17 anti-submarine strike aircraft. Having to show my brand-new security
pass, complete with photograph, each time I went in, allowed me to think that I was moving
into a highly secretive high-tech world. James Bond (had he then existed) would have had
nothing on this.

    As explained to me at the time, this project, soon to be named the Gannet, was the first
British 'weapons concept' machine. This meant that the airframe and stores – i.e. weapons
– it was required to carry were integrated from day one. I was given to understand that
prior to the Gannet, although aircraft were designed for a specific purpose, the weaponry
was fitted into what space the airframe allowed. Even though I found that hard to believe,
it was an explanation given to me by Cyril Scott, the senior designer in charge of weapons
installation, so who was I, in my very junior capacity, to query it. What did impress me

An early concession to the 'paperless office' was the lofting department's transfer of data from the draughtsmen's original drawings on to aluminium sheets. These were then photographically reproduced as manufacturing templates. (Fairey Archive)

was the clever coupling of two Armstrong Siddeley Mamba propeller-turbines, which, driving contra-rotating propellers through coaxial shafts, provided twin-engine safety and range but with the reduced frontal area drag of a single-engine machine. A conventional twin-engine design would have increased the Gannet's wing span thus causing shipboard accommodation problems when having to cope with the Royal Navy carriers' existing lifts.

After a protracted trials period, which saw the Gannet selected over the Blackburn Y.B.1, the first Fleet Air Arm squadron to receive them – No 826 – was formed in January 1955, and the type eventually replaced the American Grumman Avengers and Douglas Skyraiders then in Royal Navy service. Various marks of Gannet flew with the German, Indonesian

Taken in the late 1950s, this picture shows the prototype Gannet A.E.W.3 on the engine run-up area for aircraft coming out of the Hayes experimental department. It also shows the close proximity of the electronics giant EMI, and the huts housing the drawing office school and the patents department. (Fairey Archive)

OFFICIAL SECRETS ACT, 1911

SECTION 1.

Penalties for Spying.

1. If any person for any purpose prejudicial to the safety or interests of the State—

(*a*) approaches or is in the neighbourhood of, or enters any prohibited place within the meaning of this Act; or

(*b*) makes any sketch, plan, model, or note which is calculated to be or might be or is intended to be directly or indirectly useful to an enemy; or

(*c*) obtains or communicates to any other person any sketch, plan, model, article, or note, or other document or information which is calculated to be or might be or is intended to be directly or indirectly useful to an enemy;

he shall be guilty of felony, and shall be liable to penal servitude for any term not less than three years and not exceeding seven years.

2. On a prosecution under this section, it shall not be necessary to show that the accused person was guilty of any particular act tending to show a purpose prejudicial to the safety or interests of the State, and, notwithstanding that no such act is proved against him, he may be convicted if, from the circumstances of the case, or his conduct, or his known character as proved, it appears that his purpose was a purpose prejudicial to the safety or interests of the State; and if any sketch, plan, model, article, note, document, or information relating to or used in any prohibited place within the meaning of this Act, or anything in such a place, is made, obtained, or communicated by any person other than a person acting under lawful authority; it shall be deemed to have been made, obtained, or communicated for a purpose prejudicial to the safety or interests of the State unless the contrary is proved.

* Complete copies of the Act are available for reference in each Foreman's office.

The author's Fairey security pass. It seemed exciting at the time. (Fairey Archive) and Royal Australian navies until they were withdrawn in the early 1970s. The Gannet was regarded by the Royal Navy's pilots as an excellent aeroplane and it was later greatly regretted that no aircraft possessing the Airborne Early Warning capability of the A.E.W.3 variant was available to serve with the British Naval Task Force in the Falklands Campaign of 1982.

The Gannet senior design team was led by chief engineer D.L. Hollis Williams and chief designer 'Charlie' Chaplin. Charlie was an undoubted character who made a life-long impression. He often turned up for work in his weekend wellies with vertical flyaway hair and pebble glasses, which added an eccentric touch. Senior staff members, which I hasten to add certainly did not include me, would then be invited into his office, the door tied back with string, to discuss the problems of the day. This was all very well, but such conversations were usually conducted while he formed an endless succession of small paper cones to poke in his ears, which everyone else found somewhat disconcerting.

My introduction to the lofting group meant that I acquired a new section leader: Arthur Foster. He and his wife Vera offered me accommodation in their home at Botwell Lane in Hayes, where I stayed for six months. No doubt due to my youthful inexperience at social adjustment, I found this – putting it kindly – to be an unsatisfactory arrangement and I later

The third prototype Gannet AS 1 with half the Double Mamba powerplant shut down. Also featured is the double-occupancy third cockpit fitted pending a final decision on crew disposition. (Fairey Archive)

Herbert 'Charlie' Chaplin was an undoubted 'character' within the Fairey design hierarchy. (Fairey Archive)

moved to other digs in Waltham Avenue, much closer to the Fairey factory. It wasn't long, however, before I realised I had swapped one problem for another, as my Scots landlady, Mrs Desmond, fought a never-ending vocal battle with her Irish husband. Two small daughters, also forever at odds with each other, added to the general cacophony as I struggled to complete my Southall Technical College Higher National Certificate homework in the same room. Somehow I managed to overcome these distractions, but I never did come to terms with the revolting sandwich lunches provided by Her Warship, which I habitually tossed into the bushes on my way to work. No doubt the wildlife tucked in, but I certainly didn't, finding more comfort in a daily Mars Bar, which, being reed-thin at the time, I hoped would fill me out a bit. How times have changed.

Eventually I started the drawing office course and found myself in the unique position of being a student apprentice alongside eleven other bright, workshop-trained apprentices who, on average, were two years ahead of me in their college education. This was quite a gap to bridge and trying to understand terms like 'secondary polar moment of inertia' in the stressing exercises required much patient help from my colleagues. In a parallel stream, an equal number of young ex-servicemen were being trained as draughtsmen in an area separated from ours by a thin partition wall. The six-month DO School experience proved demanding, not only for me, but for all the other young bucks on the course. One was only allowed to drop a marking of less than 70 per cent on three of the many design exercises before being dumped off the course. Can anyone imagine company training of such importance being assessed in this simplistic way now? I'm given to understand that any such failures these days are subjected to intense psychometric analysis with due allowances made for suspected racial discrimination, underprivileged childhood, lack of proper potty training, the general state of the world economy and other such considerations.

The only picture taken within the drawing office school shows our service trainee colleagues on the other side of the dividing screen. Though a poor reproduction, the exercise shows the intersection of a radio mast with a double curvature cockpit canopy. The aim was to determine the position, size and shape of the hole in the Perspex canopy. The geometry required would defeat me now. (Bryan Hope Collection)

Everyone failed the first exercise which involved the apparently simple task of bisecting a straight line. No problem, we all thought, just swing the compass arcs from both ends of the horizontal line and where they intersect, drop a vertical. Not so. None of us had envisaged the instructors' underhand trick of looking at our attempts under a huge magnifying glass and our relatively casual attempts were harshly (but rightly) judged to be downright careless. Coming from the lofting department, where precision was paramount, I should have known better, but as a deliberate wake-up call it proved highly effective. After the first day and with now only two exercises left, our attitudes towards establishing geometric and mathematical accuracy were instantly sharpened. The transition from this first easy exercise to that of the complex stressing of an aircraft's wing-fold mechanism indicates the quality of draughtsmanship and technical understanding required before we were finally allowed to transfer to the design office. During the course I relied heavily on one or two fellow sufferers, Ted Roadnight and Mike Baker in particular, who, though now both sadly deceased, went on to hold high positions within the industry.

The two course instructors fell into what would, in today's jargon, be termed a typical 'good cop, bad cop' pairing. Frank Foster was a crew-cutted, tight-knit distanced individual

Ted Roadnight (left) and Mike Baker were exceptionally clever drawing office colleagues who went on to achieve high technical positions at Westland Helicopters and the Civil Aviation Authority in New Zealand.

who seemed determined to highlight student shortcomings. This might best be illustrated by his discouraging comment to (I think) the only other course survivor, Bryan Hope: 'It's mistakes by people like you that cause pilots to die.' What could one say to that kind of remark? On the other hand, his assistant, Tom Peel, was a warm-hearted Geordie whose lectures and sympathetic understanding made us feel that we were worth encouraging and able to make the grade.

At the end of the course, a list appeared showing our various allocations. Mine was to the relatively unexciting Gannet cockpit layout group as a then fully fledged junior draughtsman. It has to be said that I had hoped for a more exotic posting to Woomera in Australia, where Fairey had an interest in guided missile development. This, however, was not to be, so I merged into the main design office as yet another 'Bill' within the Ernie Norris empire.

It was customary in those days for draughtsmen's outings to take place once or twice a year. These usually consisted of a coachload of technical types heading off for a well-lubricated weekend at another aircraft firm, with a factory tour on the Saturday morning. The first one I experienced was to the Isle of Wight, where in 1952 the Saunders Roe Company was engaged in building the massive Princess flying boat. For some reason I, along with two

Distance, they say, lends enchantment and I had hoped to be sent to the Woomera missile testing range in Australia, where Fairey was engaged in rocket-propelled aircraft development. Here, a Fairey Delta Wing research vehicle looks purposeful. (Fairey Archive)

others – Ken Baillie (more about him shortly) and Jim Elderfield – elected to find our own way to Waterloo in order to catch the boat train down to Portsmouth. The rest of the party had the misfortune to suffer a long delay when their tube train connection to Waterloo broke down. They then had to wait until the first boat went over to the island very early the following morning, along with the daily newspapers.

Meanwhile, we three happy wanderers, well anaesthetised by whisky and brown ale and feeling no pain, proceeded by train, boat and island bus from Ryde to the Saunders Roe Sports and Social Club at Cowes. The size and calibre of the welcoming party, which included the company's chief designer Maurice Brennan, came as a bit of a shock; and I daresay our appearance was too to those expecting a larger and more circumspect contingent from Fairey. To have this pitiful trio turn up did not go down well, not least because with food rationing still in place, some personal sacrifices had clearly been made regarding the catering. I vaguely remember thankfully retreating at the end of the evening to the St Thomas' Guest House, the drumming of square dancing feet still beating my brains out, where oblivion blissfully awaited. My two colleagues settled into single camp beds, while I enjoyed the luxury of a double bed, all of which were tightly packed into a single room. It was only when we came down to breakfast that I found out I had been expected to share the bed with another chap from the main party, who, after its eventual arrival, had been prevented from getting into the room because I had put a chair under the door handle. Although the visit had got off to an unfortunate start, the sight of the gigantic Princess made one proud to be in the same industry. Whether the industry was particularly proud of us, one might well wonder.

Saunders Roe had clearly produced a most awesome machine and its sheer size, like that of its contemporary, the Bristol Brabazon, had led those of us too junior to be aware of the technical and political problems it already faced to think it must be a winner. I do recall a

Now look at that! The first Princess is brought out of the Cowes assembly shop with tail well down to clear the door structure.

story going round at the time that the heavily salt-laden sea air had caused a greater reaction than expected on the engine propeller blades and had induced them to bend forwards. This revelation had, it was said, been deduced by a local amateur analyst and not by the propeller suppliers' professional stress engineers, so I found it rather hard to believe.

Convinced that air travel would still be restricted to the privileged few and conducted in Imperial Airways pre-war-style luxury, Saunders Roe had gambled massively on the Princess to lead the way. They were not alone in their approach, for both Shorts, with the Shetland, and Blackburn, with its projected Clydesman – both huge flying boats – were confident that the future of air transport involved super-sized waterborne machines. This assumption was to prove a miscalculation on the grandest scale. Whereas during the 1930s virtually all airfields were grass-covered and able to cope with limited airline traffic, large numbers of paved runways had been created during the war which, being closer to the main cities, allowed quick passenger transfers and wiped out the previous dependence on coastal facilities. It was a sight that brought gasps of amazement from the crowds and gushing praise

Despite many suggestions for their further use, the three Princesses remained cocooned before their final journey to a scrapyard in Southampton in the mid-1960s. (Charles E. Brown Collection)

Once in the air, the Princess, with a wingspan (with floats raised) of 219ft 6in, looked truly magnificent. It was, however, beyond its time and doomed to commercial failure. (Saunders Roe Archive)

from the Society of British Aircraft Constructors' commentator Oliver Stewart, when test pilot Geoffrey Tyson flew sedately down the flight line at the 1952 and 1953 Farnborough air shows; yet the Princess's days, along with those of the Bristol Brabazon, were already numbered. Of the three built, only the first prototype, G-ALUN, made it into the air.

Tyson was also admired for flying the Saro SR.A/1 flying boat jet fighter inverted down the length of the Farnborough runway, a skill he had perfected before the war when he had become the chief aerobatic pilot with Sir Alan Cobham's Flying Circus. On one 'Circus' occasion he had had to attend court for having flown inverted down Carlisle High Street below the height of the tallest buildings. When called upon to answer a charge of dangerous flying, he stated that this was the usual way the Circus announced its arrival. This wasn't strictly true, but it was convincing enough for the magistrates, and he was let off with a nominal fine.

It was in May 1952 that a BOAC de Havilland Comet, flying between London and Johannesburg, provided the world's first jet-powered airliner service. Though this achievement promised a bright new dawn for British aviation, a series of tragic inflight

The Bristol Brabazon with a wingspan of 230ft was, with the Princess, a dramatic example of 1940s technology being overtaken by the emerging jet age. (Charles E. Brown Collection)

structural failures saw hopes dashed and the initiative passed to the American Boeing Airplane Company, with the introduction of the 707 airliner. Little did I think at the time that the Seattle-based company would feature so largely in my future career.

I had, meanwhile, become a technical assistant in the Fairey Company's patents department headed by Les Hayward. Already in the department and senior to me by five years was Ken Baillie, a tall, handsome young chap and the owner of an MG sports car, all of which left me holding a very poor hand of social cards. Notwithstanding this, we became the closest of friends, and remain so to this day. Another member of the department was O.W.H. Cooke. I only ever addressed him as Cookie, but my main recollection of him is as a member of the pre-war de Havilland sales team, the one-time owner of a Bentley 4-litre car, spending the first hour (at least) of each day doing *The Times* crossword, calling everybody 'old boy' and being an opinionated 'square peg in a round hole'. He was, however, thought to have had a tenuous link with the Fairey family, which made his eventual dismissal by Ken, when later running the department, a difficult and embarrassing business.

Our jobs were simple enough. A bright idea emanating from anywhere in the factory had to be searched for 'prior application' at the Patent Office in London, before legal protection could be set in train via the company's patent agents. Accordingly, both Ken and I were

The de Havilland Comet, which first flew on 27 July 1949, was Britain's pioneering pointer to jet-powered passenger travel. This is the second Mk I prototype, G-ALZK. (*Aeroplane Magazine*)

tasked with this form of research. One promising idea that was soon to prove troublesome to the company was a method of airframe construction called 'envelope tooling'. This reversed the conventional way of building aeroplanes where the outer skin was finally added to the inner framework. With the new Fairey system the skin plating and internal structure were assembled using pre-drilled templates located in jigs shaped to the aircraft's outer profile. To protect this seemingly advantageous process, a patent was taken out which proved to be a little too clever for its own good. Its prime claim was that the structure was held in the jig *throughout* its manufacture, but attempts to sell the system to other companies soon ground to a halt after a Shorts employee pointed out that it was only necessary to remove the said structure to fit a bracket, for example, to get round the word 'throughout'. As with the geodetic system of construction pioneered by Barnes Wallis at Vickers in the 1930s, the envelope tooling method did not revolutionise aircraft manufacture and was limited to the Gannet production line.

Patent department affairs took a different turn when, in 1953, the coronation year, Les Hayward took on the added mantle of commercial engineer. This saw the department closely allied to the firm's new moulded plastics business in trying to capitalise on the coronation 'tat' market. Picture frames, toilet seats, miners' helmets and key rings – if

Fairey had great hopes for the 'envelope tooling' method of aircraft construction. Used solely for Gannet assembly, it never gained favour with other companies in the industry. (Fairey Archive)

it had a market potential, Les Hayward was keen to promote it. I accompanied him on several excursions to London's East End in attempts to find 'spiv' sales outlets for these ghastly products. Who, one might ask, would want a toilet seat cover emblazoned with the royal coat of arms? But this commercial deviation was not allowing me to follow the aviation path I had signed up for, and, aged 21, with my military deferment due to technical studies about to expire, National Service seemed to offer an attractive alternative.

But this runs well ahead of Easter 1952 when, on a return visit to Bridlington, and with my earlier romantic association not having survived the separation, I had met at The Spa ballroom, and been totally captivated by, Miss Thelma Holbrook. After walking her home and engaging in a first kiss alongside the Priory Church wall, our mutual attraction was such that the return journey south a couple of days later proved quite a wrench. Six weeks later, on the Whitsuntide holiday weekend, I managed to fly up from White Waltham in Berkshire to Speeton airfield courtesy of a pilot friend, Butch Cooper. So far so good, but after this impressive arrival on the Friday evening, and having been met by Thelma, we discovered the following morning that a local flying club Auster had run into the starboard wing of our machine. After encountering the main spar, the intruder's propeller had shed a blade which had speared through our passenger cabin door. This naturally caused a bit of a mess, which had poor Butch wondering how on his return he could convince Fairey's chief test pilot, Gordon Slade, that he was entirely blameless for the accident. Not too deterred by the problem, which fortunately had left an expensive ground-surveying camera in the rear of the cabin intact, the local club members set to; they dismantled the damaged cream-painted wing of our aeroplane and replaced it with a silver wing from one of their own. It was in carrying out a test flight to prove the integrity of the repair that Thelma, questionably willing, undertook her first flight. Well, somebody had to do it and it did allow her to sit more or less alongside Amy Johnson as a Yorkshire aviatrix. By then, I should add, we had become an 'item'.

The mention of flying brings to mind a competition held that same year at the local cinema in Hayes. It required keen aeroplane spotters to note the machines *not* commented on in the soundtrack to the film *Flight*, narrated by the then famous broadcaster Eamonn Andrews. Ken Baillie and I went along on separate evenings and, after comparing notes, sent in a single entry. To our great surprise we won a trip for two in a Silver City Airways Bristol Freighter from Lympne in Kent to Le Touquet. This, however, presented a bit of a problem. The prize only covered the flights to and from France and, coming as it did in late September, it found us with whatever slim funds we had allocated to holidays already spent. But we were determined not to be denied our first trip abroad and somehow we managed to scrape together enough to get by. Our flight over the Channel, exciting though it was at the time, couldn't be classed as luxurious. Seated in the clamshell-door nose compartment, we were denied a window seat for the simple reason that there weren't any windows in that particular section of the fuselage. A large axe secured on the bulkhead above our heads constituted a primitive aid to escape, but being young and adventurous we didn't worry about things like that. We were going overseas. Still, it was a good job we hadn't won a trip to New York. Now, before readers of a technical disposition start to jump up and down,

This Auster Autocrat J1 G-AGXU suffered a mishap after flying me up from White Waltham to Speeton Airfield near Bridlington in 1952. Still airworthy, it has the unrecorded distinction of having given my then new girlfriend Thelma her first flight. (Peter Amos Collection)

I *know* that a Bristol Freighter couldn't cross the Atlantic, but I'm pointing a whimsical finger here at today's exacting flight requirements.

On emerging from our metal cocoon, we found that the French summer season had ended and everywhere in Le Touquet was effectively boarded up. With everyone of means having departed for the sunny south, it left us seemingly bereft of any *entente cordiale*, playing cricket using stones and a piece of driftwood for a bat, on a deserted windswept beach. This was not quite the playground of the rich we had imagined. But as we wondered what on earth to do and where to stay, considering our inadequate funds, one or two individuals appeared whose command of English fell well short of understanding Ken's only French phrase: 'How much is that key ring?' Probably thinking we were British Army deserters belatedly surfacing seven years after the Libération, their curiosity overcame the conversational difficulties and they installed us in the local hostelry. Copious amounts of the native brew, whatever it was, lubricated the evening, the highlight of which was a demonstration of wine-glass eating by Eduardo, a strange character who insisted that after each crunched mouthful we inspect his blackened set of tuskers. Entertaining though this was, both Ken and I realised with growing concern that some payment was expected. So, pleading travel fatigue (jet lag, had it then been identified, would hardly have been a term applicable to a half-hour flight in a Bristol Freighter), we retired to our room to consider our exit strategy.

The following day our hosts, ahead of any quick departures we had in mind, insisted on taking us to the weekend's chief event: a football match at Étaples. This was all very interesting, but by now we could see a serious imbalance building up between cash owing for our enforced entertainment and zero cash available. Accordingly, at an early dawn moment, we took off in true Colditz-escapee style and hitched a lift in the back of a *camion* as far as Boulogne. Unable to see the sights (there weren't any), we spent our time playing the locals at darts in Peg's Place before deciding to cut our losses and return early to England's welcoming shores. Once home, our venture ended on a particularly sad note, for it coincided with the terrible Underground disaster at Wealdstone that took so many lives and put our trivial experiences into proper perspective.

In September 1952 Thelma, unable to accept a place at either Oxford or Cambridge universities due to financial reasons, was awarded a private scholarship to Catherine Judson's Secretarial College in London's Notting Hill, before subsequently finding employment at the BBC. Residing at a sedate ladies' residential establishment in Holland Park, her move down south allowed our relationship to flourish and though forever strapped for cash, I somehow managed to travel from Hayes twice a week for a romantic visit. Love conquers all, they say, and this routine continued until my eventual call-up for National Service in September 1954. The general lack of money was to some extent offset by my playing, what is now termed, 'tweny-tweny' (*sic*) cricket at the weekends for Fairey, and during the evenings in the firm's interdepartmental competition. Perhaps the most impressive-sounding team we

Perhaps not the fastest thing in the sky, but the Bristol Type 170 Freighter carried Ken Baillie and I from Lympne to Le Touquet on our first overseas flight. It even got us back as well. (Bristol Archive)

Ken, being rather tall, only just made it through the clamshell-type nose opening.

came up against was the Royal Household at Windsor Castle, although on the two occasions I played there Prince Philip failed to put in an appearance. Supposedly an avid cricket lover, I assumed that he, having learned of our fearsome reputation, had belatedly remembered other public events that required his attendance. Rather a poor show, I thought, after having twice packed a clean shirt and specially whitened my boots. The Duke of Edinburgh did, nevertheless, visit the firm but that was too late for me. I'd already accepted his wife's invitation to join the RAF.

My northern presence in the Fairey cricket teams frequently generated much good-natured banter regarding the contrasting batting styles of Len Hutton and Denis Compton. I always knew I was in for a lot of flak if either Len or myself, acting unknown to him as his southern-based torchbearer, failed to produce the goods. On one occasion the great man came down to give a lecture in, of all places, the Fairey works canteen. It was totally packed out, but I did, with nervous dry throat, manage to croak out the question, 'What was your favourite ground?' Contrary to my expectations of the Oval or Headingley, he replied that it was Bramall Lane in Sheffield, which eventually hosted its last Yorkshire cricket match in 1973, as the county drew with the old rival Lancashire.

As a semi-willing cricket spectator, Thelma frequently paid a heavy price when, as so often happened, the weather turned cold or damp, or a grumpy batsman (me, can you believe)

The personal standard of the Duke of Edinburgh flies over the company during his visit to Hayes in 1955. (Fairey Archive)

Sir Richard Fairey greets HRH The Duke of Edinburgh on his arrival at the company. (Fairey Archive)

Off the back foot! Taken in Windsor Great Park when warming up to play the Royal Household, this is my only opportunity to get on the same page as Yorkshire's Len Hutton.

Len Hutton posing at Scarborough in 1948. I don't imagine he was smiling after being bowled out by Australia's Ray Lindwall for 0 just before a sea fog stopped play for the day.

The Fairey Aviation drawing office interdepartmental cricket team in 1952. I am seated next to the patents department head, Les Hayward, on the left of the picture. Ken Baillie is the good-looking guy in the middle of the back row.

made a low score. I must admit that the hours she spent patrolling the boundary must have seemed endless and hardly helped to make for a happy day, but there were many good ones, too. Somehow we got by, but cricket, though a well-meaning-enough pastime, will always prove to be the true test of a relationship.

When the time came for me to give serious consideration to National Service, my first thought was to try for an aircrew commission in the Fleet Air Arm. The selection process involved an initial weeding-out of candidates at RAF Hornchurch. This was followed by a more rigorous testing phase at Lee-on-Solent. It was here that, after passing all the aptitude, general intelligence and initiative tests, a fair proportion of attendees, including myself, were failed due to colour-blindness. I remember a surgeon commander saying, 'Well, son, I shouldn't worry too much. I've probably saved your neck for you!' Though not much consolation at the time he was probably right, but I've never figured out why, with so many candidates rejected for this deficiency, it wasn't discovered at the start of the selection process rather than at the end. Within days of this finding, the national recruiting system took over and I was quickly informed that, despite my unfortunate shortcoming, the queen was still highly desirous of my company at RAF Cardington for 'kitting out'. Most considerately, she even sent the one-way fare!

4

'EYES RIGHT THAT AIRMAN'

The Church Lads Brigade hadn't quite prepared me for the cultural shock of National Service. I suspect that few young men were prepared, but I later came to understand that a military system simply has to break down and reassemble an individual's mental and physical make-up in order for it to work. Such a realisation wasn't apparent to many at the time and, as experienced by conscripted men the world over for hundreds of years, the transition from civilian life frequently proved difficult. To find some cretin empowered to shout obscenities in your ear while you stood rigidly to attention, unable to respond, was soul-destroying at the time, but was soon regarded as a rite of passage that we all had to undergo. 'Never have so many been shouted at by so few, for so long, to such little purpose' seemed to paraphrase Winston Churchill's famous epithet pretty well. Some survived it better than others, but having become well accustomed to life away from home, I found it easier than some to adapt to my new enforced environment.

My first sight of RAF West Kirby, near Liverpool. Exuding a calm and relaxed atmosphere, its resident drill corporals did everything possible to ensure one's eight-week stay was memorable.

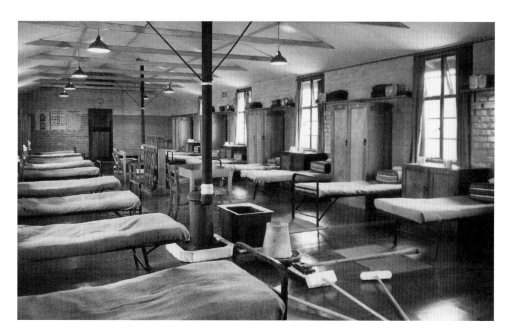

Notice the attention to accommodation cleanliness encouraged by the friendly NCOs. No need for anyone to feel lonely or neglected here.

After the basic indoctrination at Cardington, we were bussed to the training camp at RAF West Kirby in Cheshire and directed into the fifteen-man huts that were to be our homes for the next eight weeks. A body of men will, within a short time, establish a pecking order, very often based on an instinctive sensing of 'those who would do' and 'those who would have it done to them'. An example of this was the instant recognition of an unsuspecting victim for the following practical joke. A metal nut was attached to a long piece of cotton thread and placed in an empty Coke bottle. The bottle was placed under the poor lad's mattress close to his head and the cotton thread led out of sight to the next bed. After lights out a suitable time was allowed to elapse before the thread was gently pulled. With no immediate response we thought our drowsy colleague had beaten us to it and was already fast asleep, but a few more jiggles brought success. 'What's that noise?' Total silence, apart from a stifled giggle on the opposite side of the room. Tinkle tinkle. 'Is anybody awake? Can't you hear it?'

By now, with much affected irritation, somebody said, 'For Chrissake, what are you on about?' to which an added voice said, 'I bet it's that rat we saw in the corridor earlier.'

'Rat! What rat?' exclaimed the victim, by now out of bed. At this point the door to the hut corporal's room at the end of the barracks burst open. On hearing there was a rat, he disappeared *tout de suite* back into his room with a 'Well, it ain't in my f***ing room so get those bloody lights out!' Now there's sympathetic understanding for you. It only remained to place a pile of chewed-up paper under his bed to convince our friend in the morning that he had, indeed, hosted a nocturnal visitor. We didn't think it fair to repeat the prank. Well, not until the next new suitable inmate turned up.

'Square bashing' at West Kirby was not to my liking, but an eventual posting to the School of Land Air Warfare at Old Sarum in Wiltshire could barely be called a hardship. Within my two years of serving the queen I reached the dizzy heights of corporal technician, heading a three-man team that produced demonstration material for the school's teaching staff. This rarely called for technical drawing skills, more for an artistic ability which, considering my adjudged colour-blindness, proved somewhat ironic. Most of the instructors were easy to get on with and, having come from the aircraft industry, I had an ace card to play when it came to talking about aeroplanes. The highly secret test establishment at Boscombe Down was only a couple of miles away as the crow flies, and I was deeply envious of anyone who had the opportunity to work on the new types being evaluated there for service use. My only reason to visit Boscombe Down, however, was to see the RAF dentist!

This was 1954, at a time when aircraft such as the Gloster Javelin, DH 110, Fairey FD.2 and many other types were constantly under test, but at Old Sarum the station 'hacks' were far more prosaic. The Anson, Oxford, DH Dominie and Chipmunk – exotic, perhaps, by today's standards – were far from exciting, but the boss's call, 'Grab a parachute, Cruddas, we're flying in twenty minutes', invariably meant a pleasant drone down to Swanage on the coast, most often in a Chipmunk or Anson. A tootle along the Dorset coastline and up Southampton Water, which often allowed me to look down the funnels of the *Queen Mary* or *Queen Elizabeth* liners docked in Southampton, was the usual pattern before Salisbury's cathedral and Old Sarum hove into sight. My flying companion, Squadron Leader Burt, would – with entirely misplaced confidence – invite me to offset the precession of the gyro compass every fifteen minutes or so and tell me to get us back to base; this was often just after throwing in a loop or two to get me totally disorientated, but I soon got the hang of it. From time to time I got the opportunity to go up in other types of aircraft. A visiting Boulton Paul Balliol provided an unusual 'side by side' training flight, but perhaps my ascent in a Sikorsky R4 helicopter, which in 1955 was a very rare bird, was the log-book entry to be envied.

The advent of the School of Land Air Warfare's first 'atomic' course in 1956 brought some added excitement. The school's usual routine involved groups of officers from many NATO countries attending conventional air defence, transport support or offensive wing courses. Red Army faces Blue Army with such and such resources allocated to each side, sort it out chaps and then line up to receive a course certificate, prepared in Gothic script by yours truly. It was virtually a production line operation. The 'atomic' element, however, brought with it massive extra security. RAF police patrols with fearsome guard dogs were everywhere, no doubt keen to flush out all those nasty Soviet agents thought to be lurking in the surrounding countryside.

Compared to today's highly advanced electronic displays, the charts we had to produce were simplistic artworks on black cartridge paper fixed to wooden battens. For example, to illustrate the movement of a radioactive cloud resulting from an atomic bomb dropped over, say, Liverpool, I would paint an X on Day One of a chart showing the country's outline and the prevailing wind direction. This was then attached to a large roller map arrangement. By gradually hand-manipulating the rollers, much like turning granny's old mangle, a succession of similar diagrams showed the progression of this terrifying monster

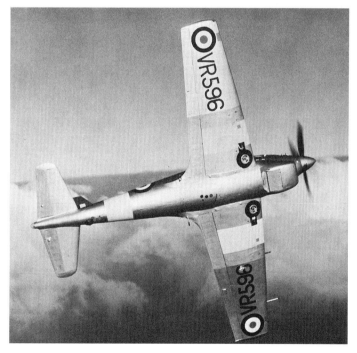

Above: The de Havilland Chipmunk T Mk 10, designed by the English firm's Canadian subsidiary, was a delightful aeroplane to fly, even in my inexperienced hands. (*BAE Systems: A Proud History in Aviation*, 2000)

Right: The Boulton Paul Balliol T 2 was already going out of RAF service before I managed a flight. Nevertheless, sitting behind its aggressive-looking 1,245hp Merlin engine gave one a distinct 'fighter boy' feeling. (*Aircraft of the RAF*, 1978)

cloud towards south-east England, assuming, that is, a north-west wind of a certain speed. With me so far? Had the wind been from the south-east, I dare say Iceland would have had more cause to be concerned. It was all a bit reminiscent of Hollywood's silent film days. Nevertheless, with the drawing office activities being hugely hush-hush at the time, it encouraged me to approach Squadron Leader Burt to request, tongue-in-cheek, a promotion in line with my 'worrying new responsibility'. Despite my demob being comfortably in sight,

The Sikorsky R4B Hoverfly was a rare visitor to Old Sarum. I was particularly lucky to have an accommodating naval pilot in 1955. (Westland Archive)

I did in fact get the 'establishment' for that particular posting raised from junior technician to corporal technician. Viewed from this distance it doesn't sound like a big deal, but to get anything like a posting establishment, that had been cast for years in service administration concrete, changed in such a short time, was a significant achievement.

Anyone who had played any kind of sport at a reasonable level had a head start in the forces. I was fortunate in that several of the officers on the instructing staff loved cricket, but without wishing to sound condescending, some were more keen than capable. This was all to the good for it led to my becoming the captain of the Old Sarum All Services XI, with a number of commissioned gentlemen, including Brigadier Weston, the assistant school commandant, and Lieutenant Commander Gilmour, under my temporary but highly respectful direction. This I regarded as only fair because, let's face it, I was under their command for the rest of the week.

As much as service rules would allow, sport was a great leveller, but there was a distinct line to be drawn between the officers and other ranks when it came to post-match 'playtime'. This usually resulted in the 'gentlemen' retiring to either the officers' mess or the appropriate bar of a familiar pub, and the 'players', funds permitting, gathering in the less formal atmosphere of the NAAFI. This was not unlike the lingering demarcation to be found in the amateur and professional status of cricketers in the county game. This social divide didn't, however, create any real problems, for had the officers' ladies been present, I think the average 'ranker' would have felt out of his depth making small talk with a senior officer's wife.

Whatever happened to the likely lads? It was my good fortune to captain a cricket team at Old Sarum that included members from all three forces. Lieutenant Commander Gilmour, wearing the blazer, and Brigadier Weston on his left were true gentlemen of the old school whom I greatly respected. Adjustments to field placings always required a 'Please, sir' to be attached. No problem in their respective cases.

There can't have been many of the out-of-the-way Wiltshire villages surrounding Salisbury at which we didn't play cricket, but I do recall Pitton, where with the steep slope of the pitch assisting my off-breaks, I was able to claim the highly improbable bowling figures of 10 for 26. As the wickets began to fall, and sensing glory, I invoked 'captain's privilege' and kept myself on; but some measure of the opposition's strength may be gained from the fact that the last man in was a young lad wearing a raincoat with man-sized pads strapped over his wellies. No matter, he stood between me and a niche in sporting history (well, in mine at least) and by golly, I got 'im. No quarter asked for and certainly none given by we hard-nosed northerners. Wellie Before Wicket! Not too many score books can claim that as an entry.

Cricket provided a wonderful introduction to the more acceptable elements of National Service life. Brigadier Weston, a pipe-smoking gentleman to the very core, gave me a ticket to the 1956 Lord's Test match that he couldn't use, complete with travel warrant; and I discovered two service policemen, a species one normally treated with excess respect, who like me spent many hours in the nets during the summer evenings. Needless to say, their friendship was worth cultivating.

One 'cricket' event did cause a bit of a problem. AC1 Roger Bellamy, then well advanced towards his demob and hence ahead of me in the drawing office pecking order, had devised a form of indoor cricket wherein a projectile, formed of hard-packed paper and encased in

Ex-National Service colleague Roger Bellamy taken in later, more prosperous years. (Roger Bellamy)

sacking and masking tape, was used to bowl at a batsman armed with a yard-long blackboard ruler. One Saturday afternoon, with the imaginary Test crowd hushed, a fierce beamer, i.e. head-high full-toss, beat my attempted pull to mid-wicket and went straight through a glass panel in the door behind me. God, what now, we thought, already seeing the inevitable Charge Form 252s being written out. The first thing was to pick out the remaining bits of glass from the frame so that it wasn't immediately obvious that government property had been carelessly damaged. The second priority was to hightail it into Salisbury in a vain attempt to find a glazier. Being a weekend, there was little chance of this and it took several days before we could coerce the station 'chippie' to produce the necessary repair materials. Strangely, despite the three-striped admin types forever in and out of the office, no one noticed the missing pane. An interesting footnote to this story is that Roger and I lost contact with each other after leaving the service; until, that is, he happened to hear my voice on a BBC television programme in 2008. Without hesitation and not even looking up at the screen, he declared to his wife, 'that's old Cruddas speaking', and a quick glance confirmed that he was right. Not a bad recall after a fifty-year separation. Roger followed up his surprise discovery with a letter to the BBC that eventually reached me and allowed a firm cementing of our service friendship.

Guard patrol duties consisted of walking round the airfield perimeter armed with what looked like a sawn-off chair leg, whistle and torch in case the perceived threat of an IRA attack on the station armoury materialised. Team selection for this tended to rely on a peculiar form of lottery. Each evening, five candidates nominated on the Station Daily Orders would parade in front of the guard room for inspection by the duty officer. Whichever one of the five he considered to be the smartest and best turned out was nominated 'stick man' and relieved of further duty. In order to stand any chance of being so regarded it was customary, nay essential, to beg, borrow or threaten one's way into acquiring the best outfit possible, which was usually a combination of ill-fitting jacket, trousers, boots, hat etc. Some of the lads were very good

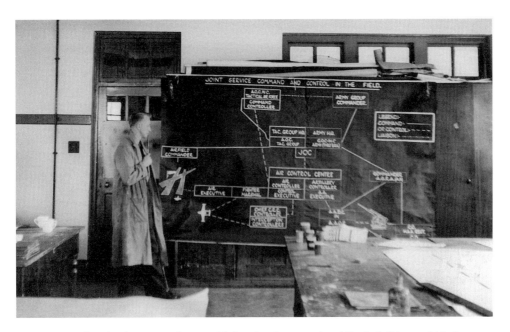

Preparing another dazzling artistic lecture aid showing Command and Control. Of more historic interest here is the door which suffered damage (suitably concealed) when a 'Bellamy beamer', lacking control of any kind, beat my intended pull shot.

This aerial picture, taken in July 1956, shows the boundary of the Old Sarum airfield. When on perimeter patrol in the middle of a wet and windy night, one hoped that the shape looming out of the dark was a colleague and not an IRA commando intent on raiding the station armoury.

Taken just before my entry into the RAF, this picture never strayed far from my locker.

at putting creases in their uniforms in the right places, but this was a skill I never excelled at, even less that of polishing boot toecaps to a mirror finish, hence my high dependency on those who did. Despite this combined effort, I can't recall ever gaining the coveted honour of 'stick man'. There was more chance of winning the VC. Fast-forwarding some sixty years, my grandson Angus, now 15 years of age, is a most enthusiastic Air Cadet bandsman who is quite addicted to the 'spit and polish' side of cadet life. What I would have given to have him as my billet companion at Old Sarum all those years ago!

Worthy of mention is that during my period at Old Sarum, in March 1956, the Fairey FD.2 supersonic delta research aircraft, based at Boscombe Down and flown by Peter Twiss, attained the World's Absolute Airspeed Record of 1,132mph flying at 38,000ft. I felt immensely proud of this company achievement and didn't hesitate to seek out Jack Hillard, the company's main technical representative, for a drink at the Old Castle Inn at Old Sarum. On one occasion, I chased on foot a Fairey Aviation van that I had spotted in Salisbury, but despite its delays at traffic lights I never caught up with it and had to admit defeat. I simply couldn't wait to get back into the professional aviation scene, but Jack always kept me informed of the trials progress at Boscombe Down. It's ironic to think that my family's Air Cadets now enjoy air experience flights from Boscombe without the faintest understanding of its place in the history of test flying. I'm working hard at putting that right.

When meagre funds allowed, a cinema visit into Salisbury provided a welcome distraction. Better still was a demob party at the aforementioned Old Castle Inn, where Thelma once came to spend a delightful week. The only drawback to attending such an event was that it was

The barrack blocks surrounding the parade square at Old Sarum were named Quetta, Peshawer, Heliopolis and Ambala, no doubt reflecting a time when the RAF had an influential presence in the Middle East. A nostalgic visit in later years revealed the square, the site of so many inspections in the past, now relegated to car park duties. No more the 'Ride of the Valkyries' or 'Sussex by the Sea' stirringly played by the band of the Parachute Regiment.

somebody else's 'do', which emphasised the fact that one's own launch back into civilian life was still way off in the future. But sure enough, to the envy of those whose 'first pay book entries were still wet', as longer-serving veterans have always pointed out, the day inevitably came, in my case on 4 September 1956, when it was time to leave the station for the last time. Not exactly with regret, I should add, because following our lengthy courtship, sustained mainly by correspondence, weekly phone calls and the all-too-infrequent passionate 'forty-eights' (forty-eight-hour passes), Thelma and I were due to be married in less than three weeks' time. 'Out of the frying pan, into the fire', the cynics used to say, but fifty-six years later, it is still the best choice I could possibly have made. This brings to mind the unfortunate experience of an RAF sergeant on the base who shinned up a drainpipe to reach the bedroom window of a girl who worked in the NAAFI below. Having almost reached his goal, the pipe came away from the wall, and so did he, breaking his leg in the process. I sometimes wonder if the CO hid a smile when listening to the poor chap's explanation, but to save further embarrassment he was posted to another station shortly after hobbling out of the sick bay. Never a dull moment.

Old Sarum, the RAF's third oldest airfield with hangars constructed by German prisoners during the First World War, was, like all the permanent RAF establishments in the

'Last Orders Please.' The guard room at Old Sarum, just prior to its demolition in 2003.

mid-1950s, a model of service efficiency, cleanliness and good order. Since that time much change has taken place and large sections have been taken over by housing and business unit development. However, light aircraft and gliders continue to fly from this historic airfield and ambitious plans are in hand to expand the newly arrived Boscombe Down Aviation Collection.

5

POST-NATIONAL SERVICE: REALITY AWAITS

After life in the services, many found readjustment to civvy street to be an extended business. In my case it took all of twenty-four hours. Just two and a half weeks after waving cheerio to all at Old Sarum, on a beautiful sunny day – 22 September 1956 – Thelma and I were married in Bridlington's Priory Church. Our honeymoon to St Ives in Cornwall was cut short by both limited funds and rainy weather, and we arrived, earlier than planned, with but £10 to start our married life, in the downstairs half of a house in Southall, a couple of miles from the Fairey factory in Hayes. While love and the resilience of youth can withstand most things, bills have to be paid and a built-in resistance to buying anything on hire purchase (heaven forbid!) meant that we lived on a shoe-string and saved in the threepenny-bit jar until we could afford to pay cash for any item.

When I first joined Fairey in 1951, some 180,000 people were employed within the British aircraft industry, but by 1956, when I re-entered as a draughtsman in the engineering development department, this number had risen to 300,000. I find it amazing now to

The happy couple outside Bridlington's Priory Church. 22 September 1956.

One of sixteen Gannets delivered to the West German Naval Air Arm in 1958. (Fairey Archive)

recall the variety of projects then being undertaken by the company. The Gannet, FD.2, Jet Gyrodyne, Ultralight helicopter and Rotodyne were all aircraft that required test rigs and it was this department that designed them, carried out the ground tests and analysed the results.

The FD.2, the last fixed-wing type to be designed and built by Fairey, was a revolutionary research aircraft which, having already exceeded the world airspeed record by 300mph, had enormous potential as a Mach 2 front-line fighter. As such, it was in contention with other British advanced projects such as the Saunders Roe 53 and 177 turbojet/rocket-propelled interceptors. In the event, none of these highly innovative aircraft passed beyond the prototype flight-testing stage. What did prove galling was the success subsequently enjoyed by the French Dassault Mirage III fighter whose wingspan and length were within inches of those of the FD.2.

The Mirage's success in both the Israeli Six-Day War with Egypt in 1967 and the Argentinian air force's performance over the Falklands in 1982, was clear proof, if indeed proof was needed, that Fairey had got the design approach spot on. However, lacking government funding, the FD.2 was denied a massive export opportunity. Yet this remarkable machine remained a showpiece vehicle for the British aircraft industry, then in the last stages of national technological independence. The first prototype, WG 774 (two were built), went on in the mid-1960s, after being fitted with a redesigned new ogive (double-curved leading edge) shaped wing by the British Aircraft Corporation, to assist the checking of Concorde's aerodynamic characteristics. It now resides alongside the second prototype Concorde (002) in the Fleet Air Arm Museum at Yeovilton.

Unfortunately, one sees history repeating itself with the announcement in February 2012 that the French Rafale, having won a large export order from India, has stolen a march over the technically superior Eurofighter. Not good news for BAE Systems' Warton factory and the associated equipment supplier companies.

Fairey's FD.2, pictured here over southern England, was, along with the company's Rotodyne, a technical achievement that failed to attain matching commercial success. (*Flight*)

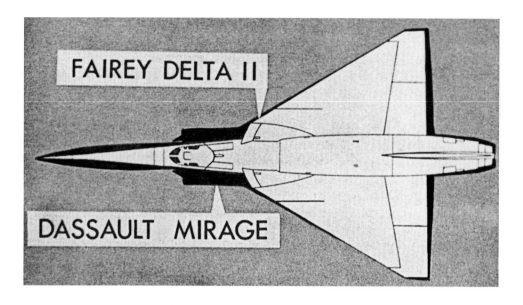

Above: The similarities between the British and French supersonic fighter design approaches are well illustrated here. (Fairey Archive)

Left: The FD.2, WG 774 was the aircraft in which Peter Twiss achieved the world airspeed record. It became the BAC 221 after modification at Filton to incorporate the ogive wing shape proposed for Concorde. The canister, with pennant, is an item of ground equipment used to protect the nose pitot. (Fairey Archive)

With all the major company project offices engaged in military aircraft studies, the 1950s produced an interesting range of designs. Many inevitably fell by the wayside but others were to prove world class. The Hawker Hunter, for example, was a thoroughbred fighter and ground attack machine from the start, while the Supermarine Swift, initially designed to meet the same specification, was beset with technical problems. Despite the ordering of two prototypes and 100 production aircraft costing £33 million, the RAF refused to accept the early Swifts for the interceptor role, but later versions were used for low-altitude, high-speed tactical reconnaissance. The description given to the Gloster Javelin as an 'all weather interceptor' was said in certain unkind columns of the press to be essentially true – providing it wasn't dark or raining! Such scathing comment was, however, unsupported as 435 machines of various marks were built for service with the RAF. One cannot deny that the British expertise that also produced the Canberra, Valiant, Victor, Vulcan and Lightning interceptor matched that of any of the contemporary design teams engaged either side of the Iron Curtain then dividing Europe.

Fairey's entry into the 'whirlybird' world began in the mid-1940s when a design team, led by Dr J.A.J. Bennett, produced a compound helicopter called the Gyrodyne. This machine used two 520hp Alvis Leonides radial engines to produce forward thrust, with lift being provided by a conventional three-bladed rotor. Two examples were built, but the first, G-AIKF, crashed after a rotor-head failure; the pilot, F.H. Dixon, and flight observer, Derek Galloway, both lost their lives. By the early 1950s the second Gyrodyne had appeared as the Jet Gyrodyne, which now featured a single Leonides engine driving two variable-pitch propellers via a gearbox and shafts through the stub wings. An extra drive to two compressors in the pylon allowed pressurised air to be fed to fuel-burning jet units at the tips of the two-bladed rotor.

The result of a research contract placed by the Ministry of Supply, the Jet Gyrodyne was designed to gain experience of tip-jet driven rotors. (Fairey Archive)

Its main purpose was to investigate the performance of the tip jet units under a Ministry of Supply experimental contract along with procedures for the Rotodyne compound helicopter. After Dr Bennett left the company to work in America, the design team was headed by Dr G.S. Hislop and Captain A.G. Forsyth, with much assistance from an Austrian engineer, Dr August Stepan.

Stepan had worked throughout the war as part of the Doblhoff team at the Weiner Neustädter Flugzeugwerke, which produced a series of VNF 342 small helicopters embodying rotor blade tip jets for use by the German navy. The story of his arrival at Fairey, along with that of his wartime colleague Count Alexander Czernin, almost warrants a book on its own. It is recorded that in the immediate post-war race to round up German scientific personnel and equipment, the Doblhoff team was 'taken over' by a specialist American unit. However, a four-man British Army team managed to infiltrate the internment compound, and while one made a show of inspecting the captured German equipment, the others evacuated the Doblhoff trio into the back of a 3-ton truck. Despite a political row which resulted in the return of the Doblhoff team to the Americans, Stepan and Czernin were eventually smuggled inside crates, in a Lockheed Hudson, to England and hence to Fairey.

Dip. Ing. August Stepan, small in stature but big in reputation, brought his wartime rotary-wing expertise to Fairey. (Westland Archive)

The Ultra-light Helicopter, designed and built in the late fifties, appeared to meet both the army and navy requirements for a simple, easy-to-dismantle machine for casualty evacuation and reconnaissance duties. A total of six were built, but following the almost inevitable withdrawal of Ministry interest, work on the project ceased in 1959. (Fairey Archive)

As can be imagined, their contribution to the Jet Gyrodyne, its direct successor the Fairey Ultra-light helicopter, and ultimately the Rotodyne was highly significant. In the light of so many design casualties it becomes almost an embarrassment to mention the additional fate of the Ultra-light helicopter. By 1956, this promising machine had demonstrated many take-offs and landings from a flat-bed truck and also the deck of a naval frigate. These tests proved that it would be ideal for multi-service reconnaissance operations, but the company found itself staring down the gun barrel of the Ministry of Supply, which for reasons of economy no longer wished to support the project. Where have we heard that before? Not much changes in the world of service procurement it seems, with high aspirations and excellent technical effort forever being negated by a lack of adequate funding and belated loss of political interest. Think of the financial fiasco surrounding the recent scrapping of the Nimrod MRA 4 aircraft, and after how many years of ministerial vacillation?

The Rotodyne was an advanced convertiplane project that featured jet units at the tips of its four 90ft-diameter blades providing vertical lift; two Napier Eland turboprops provided the necessary thrust for forward flight. At first, this concept was thought to be the ideal answer to intercity travel and was well received by British European Airways and other potential operators. However, the aircraft's excessive noise levels and escalating development costs became the main factors that led to its eventual cancellation.

In the early 1960s the government decided to rationalise its policy regarding rotary-wing activities by placing them all under the control of Westland Helicopters or, as one magazine

The Fairey Rotodyne was based on a revolutionary design principle that is today gaining a new lease of life. Although an impressive sight in flight, the noise it generated was considered unacceptable for inter-city operations. In 1962 both the Rotodyne and the Fairey company faded into history.
(Fairey Archive)

unkindly referred to them, 'Wasteland Helicopters'. This decision undoubtedly became the straw that finally broke the Fairey Company's back, and its aircraft interests then quickly faded – as did those of many other pioneering firms – into the pages of aviation history. The merging of helicopter interests caused considerable unrest and bitterness at firms like Saunders Roe, Cierva, Bristol and, of course, Fairey, which as recently as the late 1950s had been considered a likely bidder not only for Westland itself, but for Blackburn Aircraft, its long-term arch-rival in naval aircraft design and supply. A striking example of loyalty to the firm was the covert action taken by some company diehards who, using paint stripper, removed the newly applied Westland logo from the Rotodyne's rotor pylon and replaced it with that of Fairey, just prior to its appearance at a Society of British Aircraft Constructors (SBAC) Show. Although a token act of emotional defiance that had understandable support from many employees, the die was firmly cast. Westland's name was quickly reapplied and the aircraft subsequently retained its new parent's revised styling, along with RAF roundels signifying a service interest; it was finally abandoned in February 1962.

Although that year saw the end of the Rotodyne, it heralded the first flight of the Vickers VC10 from Brooklands. Though not within my own working experience, it is of note that this company had also suffered a profound disappointment when, in 1956, its highly innovative civil airliner, the V 1000, was cancelled. With the prototype at an advanced stage of manufacture, the project followed the all-too-frequent sequence of perceived requirement (civil or military), preliminary backing and cautious financial support, before the axe fell during prototype construction. This oft-repeated pattern of events suggests either inherent monumental incompetence at the highest levels of successive governments and their military staff equivalents, or that predicting future needs is just too complicated for anyone to do accurately. I suspect a fair mixture of both.

Despite carrying out interesting work on test rig design for the Rotodyne and figuring out ways to transport the fuselage from Hayes to the test airfield at White Waltham, my two years spent at Fairey after National Service offered little hope of career or financial advancement. Thelma and I were both earning a wage, but still there was no chance of saving enough money for a home deposit. We did, however, manage to buy, for the princely sum of £30, our first car – a 1936 Austin Ten; but unable to afford driving lessons, I made the chancy and unlawful decision to teach myself to drive. Fortunately I passed the formal test first time, as did Thelma after exposure to my supposed 'expert' tuition. Not a route I would advise anyone to take today.

6

BROUGH ENCOUNTER

In 1958 an advertisement appeared seeking design personnel to work on an exciting new project at the Blackburn and General Aircraft Company at Brough. At that time the company was mainly occupied with the Beverley transport and its only jet aircraft experience had been the construction, under contract from Handley Page, of the sole HP.88 research aircraft. This was a single-seat machine with wings featuring three different degrees of sweepback attached to an Attacker fighter's fuselage. Intended for testing the Victor bomber's crescent wing shape, a number of flights were undertaken from Carnaby, but soon after delivery to Handley Page it disintegrated in the air causing the death of test pilot D.J.P. Broomfield. I saw it fly on one occasion while on holiday in Bridlington in 1951, but had no idea then as to what it was, though its unique appearance certainly aroused my curiosity. Now, with the advertisement referring to a new project, I assumed it was some later derivative of this aircraft.

There has always been a reluctance by southern folk to move north (except as an invading force), and for a present-day example, one need look no further than the BBC's effort to reposition staff to Salford in Lancashire. But to both Thelma and myself the increased salary being offered, along with a £300 interest-free loan sufficient to cover a housing deposit and legal costs, provided a heaven-sent opportunity to return to home pastures. I couldn't pen the application fast enough. It also encouraged me, having worked alongside the 'slide-rule technical types' at Fairey, to move off the drawing board and take on more analytical work as a systems engineer. Though it was almost considered treason to move to Blackburn's, I passed this off with my Fairey colleagues as a reward for having served as a modern missionary but now it was time to leave the southern heathens to their fate. I added that I had to report home for training to meet more demanding challenges. There were hoots of derision and 'Total bullshit, Cruddas. Bugger off!' So I did.

My application having proved successful, I joined the Systems Group whose efforts were concerned with the company's new project (which was in no way connected with the HP.88). This was a Low Level Strike bomber for naval use and referred to as the NA.39. I was immediately teamed up with a bright Scots graduate, Blair McDonald, concentrating on three separate areas of development: the fuel system, armament installation and crew ejection. This involved a good deal of interfacing with the flight test team at Holme-on-Spalding Moor some 20 miles distant. By 1961, with the flight test programme fully under way, I was transferred full time to the airfield, whereupon I became the senior systems engineer in

Time to head
north, but not
without a delicate
leg glance
as a parting
shot. Technical
Publications artist
Ian Huntley (now
deceased) created
this cover for my
Fairey farewell
card.

charge of fluid/mechanical systems flight testing on what had by then become the Buccaneer. Twenty aircraft were allocated to the pre-production testing of this advanced aircraft, which seemed a large number at the time, but which permitted aerodynamic and systems testing, engine development work, deck-landing tests and the evaluation of weapons carriage to be conducted in the shortest timescale. Sadly, however, eight of this development batch were lost, along with some of the test crews; flying accidents were all too often associated with the aircraft due to it initially being fitted with de Havilland Gyron Junior engines which were seriously underpowered.

Although the design and service history of the Buccaneer is well recorded elsewhere, this may well be the place to recall one or two events that caused some hilarity, though not necessarily to all of the main participants. One of the test requirements called for a jettison system that could safely discharge fuel away from the aircraft within a prescribed flight envelope. This was not as easy as might be thought because there was a limited area behind the engine jet exhausts in which to position a suitable exit point. It was vitally important that ejected fuel did not find its way into the aircraft's radio bay within the rear fuselage or, if the airbrakes were deployed, that lubricant was not washed off the extension mechanism. It was also thought that there might be a risk of hot engine exhaust gas igniting the fuel vapour – not unlike the flamboyant performances provided at air shows by American F-III pilots to give the crowds a spectacular thrill. In order to discover the best location it was decided to install a pressurised tank inside the rear fuselage containing water mixed with a scarlet dye, and to link it to the mast housing the jettison outlet. The whole of the rear fuselage outer skin was also coated with white distemper. It was then a simple matter of evacuating the test tank contents during a series of flight conditions and to note, after landing, any contaminated areas on the skin surface. This procedure required somebody to enter the

An underside view showing the Buccaneer's rotatable bomb-door and the fuel jettison and tank vent outlets above the stowed arrester hook. Fixing its location required several flights with the rear fuselage coated in washable white distemper, ready to receive coloured dye from the mast outlet. (Rick Phillips/Buccaneer Aircrew Association)

restricted equipment bay to prime the test tank prior to each flight. Unfortunately (that dreaded word), on one occasion the tank, having reached full pressure, shed its connection to the mast and sprayed its contents over the poor technician, Doug Nightingale, who had no means of making a quick exit. When he did finally emerge, he was greeted with 'Hey, look! Father Christmas is bloody early this year'. As I say, not everyone saw the funny side.

As with all development, some problems proved knottier than others and one which caused me a good many midnight hours of testing was why, after an airbrake selection – which was a purely hydraulic operation – both the instruments measuring fuel flow to the engines began to oscillate wildly. Part of the investigation required the setting up of a ground test rig which featured clear polythene pipes that allowed flow behaviour to be observed. Yes, you've probably guessed it already; a pipe detached itself under full pressure to provide a most impressive fountain of fuel spurting several feet into the air. Unfortunately (again), the fuel, being indiscriminate, cascaded down on the senior design hierarchy who had chosen that particular demonstration to witness at first hand. Aviation fuel is strong-smelling stuff at the best of times and certainly not a substance to be in contact with unless suitably clothed. These gentlemen were not so clad and they failed to see anything amusing whatsoever in the situation. Neither did I when later called upon to explain to John Howland, the head man at

Holme, who was responsible for such an embarrassing cock-up. As I had been running that particular test, I didn't escape his withering comments and I left his office convinced that I had entered a lengthy period of 'negative career advancement'. Fortunately, where people are concerned, there is always the possibility that others will make mistakes bigger than one's own, and so it proved, with other flight test problems soon eclipsing my mishap. One has only to witness how, in today's political arena, seemingly calamitous situations are soon overtaken by the latest shocking event or bigger and better scandal.

The winter of 1962/63 was very severe; indeed, the coldest on record and it's difficult now to recall that the houses we regarded with such pride were still, in the main, coal-fired with perhaps a single-bar electric heater in the bathroom. This 'luxury', however, invariably failed to prevent icy crystals forming on the inside of the windows in the morning. A perishing thought these days, but another fact of life one simply put up with, along with frequently having to get one's car started by putting the distributor cap and plug leads in the oven for a warm-up. Most people seemed to have similar problems which we all learned to take in our stride.

In February 1963 I was called upon to join HMS *Ark Royal* as a technical representative when 801 Squadron embarked with its Buccaneer S. Mk 1s at Devonport. This was my first introduction to life on the high seas, and during a week of bitter weather in the English Channel, I gained an immense admiration for the flight and ground crews who managed to launch, fly and recover the aircraft in such cold and unbelievably noisy conditions. Each evening my presence was expected in the wardroom for dinner. Not at the time possessing my own dinner jacket ensemble, I had been kitted out prior to departure by well-meaning

An 801 Sqn Buccaneer S. Mk 1 generates full thrust on *Ark Royal*'s catapult. Very noisy and very cold! (Rick Phillips/Buccaneer Aircrew Association)

colleagues; they loaned me various items that more or less fitted, provided one didn't look too closely. My strangulated plea for help in trying to fasten a bow tie into a collar two sizes too small caused much amusement and a less-than-reassuring, 'You'll get by'. I wasn't convinced. Memories of my unsuccessful attempts to win 'stick man' approval rose rapidly to the fore.

'Pink gin, sir?' Oh, Christ, if only this damn ship would stay still for a moment I would really fancy one, but 'Yes, please, put it down there, I'll find it later' might have summarised a typical evening's conversation as I manfully struggled to defer an instant re-acquaintance with my dinner. Each evening's meal brought with it lots of interesting naval-related chat, but not being at my social peak, I doubt that my contribution impressed the assembly of young officers heartily tucking in. 'Where's my bunk?' was a question I asked more than once as the mighty *Ark* ploughed on, regardless of my discomfort. At one point, she mercifully hove to in Weymouth Bay, whereupon a horde of ratings disappeared over the side to play football against local teams. I also took advantage of the welcome break and journeyed landward to enjoy a more stable walk along the town's promenade. Yet when it was time to re-embark, I in my 'civvies', along with two teams of extremely muddied players, found myself vying to be first up the rope and scaffold tubing ladder back on to the deck. Unfortunately for the esteemed Commander Mike Crosley RN, while leaping from the cutter on to the ladder he let go of his briefcase which disappeared into the briny. No call for that kind of language, sir, *please*!

A successful launch. With pilot 'hands off', and amidst flurries of steam, the catapult takes over. (Rick Phillips/Buccaneer Aircrew Association)

With the Buccaneer safely airborne, the strop falls into the Channel. No way was ever devised for saving these items. The pilot was by this stage in full control. (Rick Phillips/ Buccaneer Aircrew Association)

Ark Royal ploughs on in foul weather – outside even the Fleet Air Arm's operating limits. (Rick Phillips/Buccaneer Aircrew Association)

As to be expected, technical problems arose on the Buccaneer now that it had entered its operational environment. Some demanded an instant answer. One such problem was the inconvenient habit of the aircraft's normal/emergency hydraulic system changeover valve reverting to 'emergency' after an arrested landing. With the valve being difficult to get at, it required time and effort to restore the settings to 'normal' that was not appreciated by the servicing crews. Clearly the unit was too 'g' sensitive, but the pointed question asked by the engineering officer was: 'What are you going to bloody well do about it? Come on, Cruddas, that's what you're here for. Sort it out PDQ. Flying tomorrow at 7 a.m.' That was all very well, and I could appreciate the urgency of a fix, but I first needed to know if this was a problem already understood back at base and if a solution was being worked on. It was arranged that the following morning I would fly to Gosport in a Whirlwind helicopter where I could contact the company's design people by landline. The technical outcome apart, what made this a memorable experience was when, with the Whirlwind's cabin door fully open just prior to lift-off, the ground crew chief appeared and shouted – and I mean shouted – 'If this f***ing thing goes down, don't all go for the same f***ing exit, and wait until you're under water before you try to get out, otherwise you'll get your f***ing heads chopped off!'

You will gather from reading this that all did in fact go well, but I later learned that the Fleet Air Arm's mortality rate at the time was, putting it mildly, uncomfortably high. The return flight to *Ark Royal* required the helicopter to hover off the port beam (note the clever use of naval terminology); and Hawker Siddeley's test pilot Bill Bedford, despite never having previously landed a combat aircraft of any kind on to a carrier, lowered the first prototype P1127, XP 831 – the forerunner of the Harrier vertical take-off aircraft – on to the deck. Later on, after blundering into the 'Heads' to find a very hairy Bedford taking a shower while standing in an antiquated Victorian bath, I couldn't help but wonder how the ship, having just emerged from a major refit at Devonport, could still retain such ancient equipment. The bath, that is, not Bedford! Stretching my imagination, I put it down to a traditional preference for Nelsonian standards of plumbing. Today I would be more inclined to blame the rigorous cuts in defence spending.

One of the tasks given to Mike Addley, the company's resident flight test observer, and myself was the cine filming of the Buccaneers as they approached the rear of the carrier. The aircraft would appear a mile or so away, usually in a grey stormy sky, flaps, arrester hook and undercarriage down, seemingly just hanging in space. We were experiencing a sensation akin to going up and down 16ft or so in a relentless lift as we tried to focus the film camera. I recall saying to Mike as we stood under the 'round down': 'We must be bloody mad doing this. If he undershoots, we are total goners.' Mike replied with typical British understatement: 'Whatever, all in a day's work.'

Opposite top: Make way, here comes Bedford! Hawker Siddeley's chief test pilot makes the first VTOL landing on a carrier, in the first prototype P1127, XP 831 on 8 February 1963. The author is aboard the Whirlwind helicopter off the port beam. (Hawker Siddeley Archive)

Bottom: Ark Royal's crew appreciate Bill Bedford's novel approach to carrier landings. (Hawker Siddeley Archive)

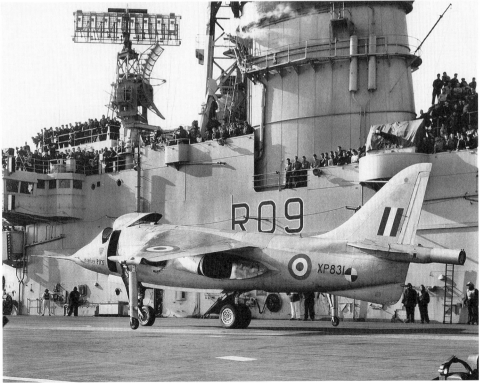

Although XP 831 is safely down on this occasion, Bedford wasn't so fortunate at the Paris Aero Show later that year, when, translating from hovering to forward flight, he rapidly lost height and crashed in front of the crowd. (Hawker Siddeley Archive)

Far too many fatal accidents attended the Buccaneer development programme. Good friends such as flight test observers John Joyce and Trevor Dunn were lost, and 'Neddy' Nightingale suffered a permanent back injury after ejecting from the first prototype, XK 486, over Market Weighton. G.R.I. 'Sailor' Parker was the pilot on that occasion but, having survived that incident, his luck ran out later on, along with that of my next-door neighbour, observer Gordon Copeman. Just three days after I returned from my *Ark Royal* venture, both were killed in a production S.1 machine, XN 952, when a 'toss bomb' manoeuvre went disastrously wrong over the snow-covered airfield at Holme-on-Spalding Moor. Having contracted flu while at sea, I was absent from work that day, but a telephone call came from the airfield asking if Thelma and I would break the news to Gordon's wife. Before we could do this, a second call asked us to delay our approach as a company team was already on its way to deal with the matter in a more formal way.

Without a doubt, my six years at Blackburn Aircraft, which in 1963 became Hawker Siddeley Aviation Ltd, then later Hawker Blackburn Division and next Hawker Siddeley Brough before finally becoming BAE Systems Brough, provided me with much-needed experience at the sharp end of aircraft development. By the end of 1965, however, the

'Sailor' Parker (top) and test observer Gordon Copeman, lost their lives on 19 February 1963 when flying a Buccaneer S. Mk 1, XN 952 over Holme-on-Spalding Moor. The development aircraft at the airfield displayed a variety of colour schemes. (Blackburn Archive)

Buccaneer test programme had entered its final phase and re-equipping the McDonnell Douglas Phantom with the Rolls-Royce Spey engine became the company's main activity. This was at a time when American staff recruitment companies began to approach British aerospace personnel as part of the so-called Brain Drain. Nevertheless, it came as a surprise when two of my team somewhat smugly asked: 'What are you going to do when we go to work for Boeing in Seattle?' Good question, but if these guys could do it, why not me? The thought opened up a whole new world of possibilities, but I was uncertain if it offered the same attraction to Thelma. Some careful persuasion by stressing the chance to broaden our experience and see some of the world soon bore dividends. Taking a 'let's try it for, say, five years' approach, we saw it as a significant opportunity, and with our two daughters, Helen and Sally, at 3½ and 1½ respectively, we considered we were flexible enough to sample the American way of life before the need for a consistent schooling regime demanded settling down. My application for employment in the US somehow leap-frogged those of the two lads who had played their cards a bit too soon, and my early acceptance allowed me, equally smugly, to say: 'See you in Seattle, boys – assuming you ever get there!' They did, but several months later, by which time I had become a veteran employee, yet again able to show them the ropes.

Buccaneer XN 975, the second S Mk 2 in the pre-production batch conducting trials with a Flight Refuelling Ltd Mk 20 air refuelling pod. Not all receiver pilots found making a refuelling connection easy. (Blackburn Archive)

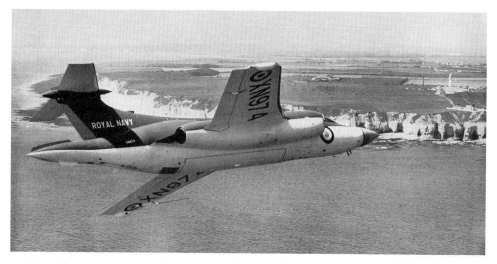

Yorkshire's best! Buccaneer XN 974, the last great British bomber, turns in over Flamborough Head – as fine a stretch of coastline as anywhere in the country. (Blackburn Archive)

My time with and departure from the Buccaneer programme coincided with the long-running political wrangling and inter-service rivalry surrounding the RAF's intended Canberra bomber replacement – the British Aircraft Corporation's TSR 2. This highly sophisticated aircraft was a miraculous outcome following the difficult integration of the English Electric Company, based at Warton in Lancashire, and Vickers-Armstrong, at Weybridge in Surrey. This unwilling merger was, however, largely instrumental in the project consuming an ever-escalating mountain of cash which the country, yet again facing severe economic problems, simply could not afford. When it was also decreed that Britain was to give up its worldwide military commitments and close down its bases east of Suez in the mid-1960s, the need fell away for an aircraft having TSR 2's promised, but then still unproven, capabilities.

One area of serious concern was that of general maintenance, as access to many components was likely to prove awkward and difficult. An Olympus engine change, for example, that was going to require three days instead of the hours stipulated by the RAF, was just one of several major hurdles still to be overcome. Despite a successful start to the flight test programme, which only extended to twenty-three flights, this advanced project was cancelled in 1966. Prior to this, much government and service debate had centred on whether the Buccaneer, if suitably modified, could offer a cheaper alternative that would be available for squadron service considerably sooner. Lord Louis Mountbatten, then chief of the defence staff, led a prolonged campaign to get the Buccaneer adopted by the RAF, and would, given every opportunity, lay down five photographs of the Buccaneer alongside one of the TSR 2 and passionately declaim, 'five of these or one of these – no contest'.

Mountbatten met formidable opposition from an air staff determined to avoid having a 'dark blue' design thrust upon them at any price. However, he had the Buccaneer bit firmly

The British Aircraft Corporation's TSR 2 promised to be a very fine race horse indeed. Unfortunately its flying start didn't go beyond twenty-three flights and the project was finally axed on 6 April 1965. (Norman Parker Collection)

between his teeth and it was thought by many that his venomous rejection of the TSR 2 finally persuaded the Australian government to abandon its lukewarm interest in placing an export order. It transpired that the Australians were already well advanced towards securing a trade deal with the Americans for the General Dynamics F-111. The British minister for defence, Denis Healey, having similar thoughts of closer co-operation with the US, also saw fit to sign an initial contract for fifty F-111Ks. This undoubtedly promised favourable financial terms and an aircraft that would, like the Buccaneer, fulfil the new less demanding requirements. But, as is well known, 'many a slip 'twixt cup and lip', and so it proved when this supposed wonder aircraft ran into severe development problems causing costs to increase almost to those of the TSR 2. This and a long delay in delivery brought about its inevitable cancellation and the introduction of the McDonnell Douglas F-4 Phantom into RAF service. The irony here, of course, is that by 1969, following the withdrawal of the Royal Navy's carriers and fixed-wing squadrons, the naval Buccaneers were transferred to the RAF where, with additional new machines delivered from Brough, they proved immensely popular with their crews and gave excellent service. They flew into well-deserved and honourable retirement in 1994.

As outlined here, the 1960s was a turbulent period for the British aircraft industry, with project disruptions following each other with predictable and depressing regularity. Therefore, it was after hearing of the additional cancellation of the Hawker P1154 V/STOL supersonic Harrier and the Armstrong Whitworth AW 681 STOL transport, and the fact that the industry seemed to be in sharp decline, that Thelma and I had made the decision to move to Seattle.

7

'WHERE YOU FOLKS AWL FROM – AUSTROYLIA?'

In the mid-1960s the American aircraft industry was facing an unprecedented skills crisis. Until then there had always been a large itinerant technical workforce willing to transport itself around the United States to wherever the latest project was taking shape. But with Boeing about to embark on its Supersonic Transport (SST), the 737 and 747 airliners, Lockheed on the L1011 TriStar and McDonnell Douglas on the DC-10, all within a year or so of each other – not to mention the military demand for, for example, helicopter gunship conversions for use in Vietnam – there became an urgent need for extra skilled personnel from overseas. It soon became clear that many of those native to the Pacific north-west had a limited understanding of the word 'overseas'. British accents, though regarded as 'kinda cute', had many guessing where Britain was located on the map, and with Australia being the next big land mass going west, Brits were usually regarded as hailing from there. Having queried with local Washingtonians why news broadcasts always dealt with city news first before moving on to state news, then national and international events – the direct opposite of the British format – it was pointed out that, 'Hell, it's only eighty years ago we were fightin' the goddam Indians up here, who needs all that other stuff?' Well, that's America for you, or at least it was in the mid-sixties. Our perceptions of America had been almost entirely influenced by films featuring slick-talking individuals living in ultra-modern homes and driving stylish convertibles. Needless to say, we in turn soon discovered that for the great majority, life was very different to that portrayed by Hollywood. Less than 5 per cent of the population held passports and few in the mid-west had visited either the east or west coast. So it was surprises all round!

American staff recruitment fell into two camps. Either one joined an established company, such as Boeing, as a permanent employee at a lower salary, or one placed oneself in the hands of a contract agency for a shorter defined period but at a much higher salary. Hoping to move around various parts of America, I opted to join Comprehensive Designers Inc. as a contract design draughtsman. Long-term company employees, I soon found out, had scant regard for home-grown 'job-shoppers', at least those at detail design draughtsman level who often lived out of the back of huge gas-guzzling cars or camper vans in parking lots close to the factory, and who moved on to another state when the accumulation of 'moving violation' tickets became too pressing. Many 'fly-by-nighters' simply upped sticks and took off, leaving unfinished drawings and no doubt unpaid bills and other debts behind. This was a revelation to me and I quickly came to understand why the Brits' more stable and flexible approach was so welcome.

Our arrival in Seattle soon prompted an example of unpremeditated goodwill, when an American family to whom we had not even spoken, seeing us dog-tired at the airport, most kindly offered to take us into their home until we sorted ourselves out. Though touched by their kind gesture, we assured them that all would be fine in the morning when my company representative was due to turn up. We then took the soft option and plumped for the Olympic, Seattle's plushest and most expensive hotel. The aforementioned rep, Fred Schnell, did duly appear, but not until three days later, by which time we had transported ourselves by bus to Renton's City Centre Motel, close to Boeing's main plant. Understandably, family relationships had, by now, become a little strained. With Thelma and I unable to figure out what on earth we had entered into, and with two small girls to placate, it wasn't the best time for this uncomprehending idiot to cheerily ask if everything was OK and was I able to report for duty at Boeing the next day. The few words that followed, which made it very clear that everything was certainly *not* OK, did little to improve an unpromising start.

Somehow, surviving the arrival experience, taking a rented house, buying a car and getting the girls into a pre-kindergarten class coincided with my becoming part of the Boeing 747 project team. In truth, this was a disappointment, for I had hoped, and indeed been half-promised, a job on the much more glamorous Supersonic Transport. But with hundreds of technicians and designers flooding in, Boeing's administration must have been

Faced with having to decide where to spend our first two nights in America, we settled for Seattle's Olympic Hotel, little realising that we had picked the most expensive hotel in town.

An Alien Gate Pass got one through the main gates into the factory. Once inside, non-US personnel were issued with a four-inch diameter candy striped badge that allowed an alien to be easily spotted from the other end of the office.

fully stretched and one had little choice but to await a job allocation. As it turned out, I was fortunate in being allocated to a company lead engineer, Ev Olsen, for scheming out the basic fuel system piping layout for the aircraft, the sheer size of which was astounding.

On 13 April 1966 Pan American World Airways announced its first order for twenty-five of the new transports and from that moment on, our two-man 'group' expanded to over seventy personnel drawn mainly from the 707 and 727 airliner design groups. In true American industrial style, the work packages were divided between highly specialised teams. What seemed to surprise Boeing's technical staff was the ability of British-trained designers and engineers who, possessing a good understanding of workshop practice, could produce drawings *and* undertake calculations to the required professional standard. In comparison to many of our American 'job-shopping' counterparts, we 'aliens' – non-Americans – were streets ahead in capability and were consequently highly valued. Balancing this, however, was the in-depth specialist skills possessed by Boeing's permanent workforce, which was extremely competent and adept at managing resources.

Establishing the sizing and location of the fuel system 'plumbing' throughout the fuselage and wings required a good knowledge of fluid performance and it occurred to me to write to Graham Marriette, the general manager at Flight Refuelling Ltd back in England with whom I had worked closely on the Buccaneer, for technical data. He suggested that rather than sending it, both he and the technical director, Mike Goodliffe, should visit Boeing and give a full presentation of the company's products. This, they hoped, would lead to a foothold in the American market, especially as the company was then hopeful of tying up a licensing agreement with Simmonds Precision Products Inc., then based in Vermont. The proposal was well received and arrangements were put in place for the fuel system specialists working on the different airliner projects to gather in a large hall. When I later asked my American group leader if a good impression had been made, he stated that there was not the slightest chance of British equipment being used on the 747 and that the sole reason for encouraging the visit was to gain insight into what developments were taking place in Europe. Not the first or last instance of British technical information taking a one-way trip across the Atlantic.

Boeing had an excellent employee educational system which offered courses on a wide variety of subjects. Being a mid-term election year, with Lyndon Baines Johnson then the incumbent president, I decided to sign up for a political awareness course which I thought would give me insight into the mysteries surrounding the Senate, Congress and the general machinations of American government. My idea was to sit at the back of the class and just listen. But no, that wasn't how it worked. Firstly, everyone in the large class had to stand up in turn and declare his or her name and reasons for attending. My announcement was greeted with enthusiasm by the class who seemed more interested in the British political set-up: many were under the impression that Britain was led on a day-to-day basis by the queen (Rupert Murdoch hadn't then appeared on the scene); others held the belief that Winston Churchill was still in charge of the country but that he had seemed a bit quiet for some time. As he had died two years earlier, aged 90, perhaps that wasn't too surprising.

I clearly had some work to do and with nowhere to hide, I was promptly appointed a discussion group leader, charged with assessing the relative merits of each country's electoral systems. This wasn't the quiet ride I had signed up for and I was hard-pressed to cope with the weight of required reading material dating back to the Declaration of Independence. One fact immediately impressed upon us was that politics is solely about power; no matter where, no matter who, no matter what. Forget the persuasive rhetoric – that's just the sugar on the pill. Dig deep enough and a politician's self-interest will emerge, and *never* trust so-called expert opinion. I thought these observations a touch cynical at the time, but another fifty years of experience has convinced me that they are essential truths, every bit as pertinent today as they were then. Less demanding but of more technical interest was the other course I enrolled on: flight operations. This gave me insight into a flight engineer's workload. A typical exercise would entail figuring out a Boeing 727's take-off configuration, including the engine pressure ratio settings, the wing flap and tailplane incidence angles, taking into account the weight of the aircraft, runway length and slope, wind direction and whether the pilot was suffering from a hangover or not (I made that last bit up). As the course progressed, various engine or system failures were introduced that kept us on our toes and convinced me that my talents (or lack of) were perhaps best kept on the ground.

Life in the American design environment could at times be a bewildering experience. In the UK I had always viewed company security as a relatively easy affair with staff arrivals each morning being a casual business. If one was visiting another company there would be a friendly indication as to where to park the car before awaiting one's contact. A few days at Boeing soon put me straight on that front. Not normally given to sporting outsize badges indicating alien status, I, along with other ex-pats, took to wearing these offensive items on the inside of our coat lapels. On one occasion, however, a revolver-equipped security guard manhandled a Brit in no uncertain manner while demanding that he display his badge – and we had a rapid rethink. This no-nonsense attitude was reinforced when some misguided individual, wishing to confront a reportedly wayward wife, gatecrashed a security entrance only to be brought to heel in a toilet area by pistol-wielding guards. This led me to think that security, American style, was the company's primary *raison d'être* and that its design people were an unfortunate overhead that just happened to produce aeroplanes.

Another surprising feature was the obsessive need-to-know culture that pervaded the design office. The lunch period was a generally perfunctory half hour which didn't allow much time for social chat, but on one occasion, and wishing to seem friendly, I moved across to enquire how my 'next-door neighbour' was getting on. As he was engaged on the 747 undercarriage retraction geometry, I could see that he had a man-sized exercise on his hands. Making conversation, I asked him how his design was progressing. He stated that it was no concern of mine! Perhaps I was just unlucky in choosing someone who was not having the requisite 'nice day'. This rebuff went along with the Americans' constant use of surnames only when addressing team colleagues in the office. It came over as downright hostile to start with, but we soon got used to it – nothing personal.

The different design groups seemed to be forever moving office or even transferring to other plant locations, but these movements were usually smooth and efficient. All kit had to be packed into large cardboard boxes (supplied) by the end of the day and clearly marked with a new mail stop location. Next day it was business as usual within an hour of starting. Most impressive.

In Seattle one is never far from the many lakes and waterways on the west coast and it was quite common for employees to turn up for work and simply hitch up their small boat, or in some cases light floatplane, to a pier or floating pontoon close to the company. Great reliance, however, was placed on the car-pooling system which, organised by a special office within Boeing, brought employees within a common area into contact with each other. The greater the number of people that shared a car, the closer to the main entrances it was allowed to park; much like the outer rings on a target converging on the centre. The difference in distance between the 'bull' and the inner and outer rings was significant, especially if one was late or it was raining, or both. Compared to British firms, US company starting times were much earlier and it was not unusual to see women driving into the car parks, perhaps having already dropped their kids off at the babysitter's house, at some unearthly hour, applying their make-up with hair still in rollers. Once out of the car it was straight to the crowded canteen for the customary coffee and doughnut. Talking of travel, I marvelled too at the office girls who delivered the vast amounts of paperwork (in those pre-email days) at high speed on roller skates down the long aisles between the drawing boards. With so much movement going on, I came to believe that with the Boeing workforce said to be around 125,000, there was only a need for around 80,000 chairs, as everyone else was in transit. Regardless, the system worked well and one quickly came to appreciate that American industry was a highly organised affair. It was also unforgiving of managerial failure.

The fuel system design group had a tightly controlled three-week timescale which required all involved to forget home life and determine system compatibility within the full-scale mock-up's cavernous wing and fuselage spaces. This called for a good deal of plea bargaining with the other specialists who had already established their system runs before it became the fuel group's turn. Group leaders had a tough time agreeing what could or couldn't be squeezed through the same lightening hole in a wing rib or fuselage frame. It was often a case of 'hard luck, buddy, we were here first, so push off and find another route'. Next was the turn of the hydraulic, air conditioning or toilet systems personnel (the latter euphemistically referred to as passenger accommodation specialists) to take over and do their bit, whereupon the wheeling and dealing started all over again. This wasn't a problem unique to the 747. Aircraft design groups have rarely had the luxury of unlimited space in which to fit equipment, after bulky items such as retracted undercarriages, fuel tanks and passenger/ bomb loads etc. have been accounted for. However, putting such trivial considerations to one side, if a 747 design group exceeded its time allowance, it was highlighted for all to see on a huge progress chart that occupied one end wall of the main assembly hall at Everett, then said to be the largest volume building in the world. On the other hand, achieving a group target was greeted with a blaring klaxon, the usual 'whoop-de-do' that goes with college football success and a large cut-out of the state's symbolic axe-carrying woodman, Paul Bunyan, being moved up the chart. It certainly wasn't like this at Brough.

One day, after a spell in the lower fuselage, I poked my head out of the mock-up's nether regions at passenger floor level to see a forest of shoes and smartly pressed trousers at calf height. One particular pair of sky-blue trousers above some fancy white shoes was markedly different to the rest and turned out to belong to the hugely popular American film star Danny Kaye, then being escorted on a tour of the works. Somehow I sensed my sudden mole-like appearance wasn't an appropriate moment to ask for his autograph.

As if that wasn't enough to get one's pulse racing, I also spent some time at the University of Washington's wind tunnel facility, pressure plotting the airflow characteristics around the 747's wing tip. This was an important exercise as it helped to determine the location of the vent exit from the fuel tanks on the underside of the wing. By way of further explanation, when an aircraft climbs to altitude, the outside air pressure decreases, the air in the tanks correspondingly expands and is spilled overboard via the vent outlet. Similarly, on descent, air is taken in through the vent until the necessary pressure balance is achieved. If the vent is incorrectly positioned, and the airflows around a wing tip can fluctuate greatly with control surface movements, pressure instability can occur that induces other problems. While on the subject, it was also necessary to build into the ramped vent arrangement a flame suppression system that would prevent a lightning strike igniting the fuel-rich mixture within the tubing leading back into the tanks. A particularly bad accident which involved a Constellation airliner's wing being blown off by a lightning strike over New York provided adequate motivation to get it right, and much analysis went into determining the various wing skin thicknesses required to resist a lightning strike-induced puncture. Aware of the vital need to be accurate with our recommendations, my Boeing lead engineer and I went over to Sea-Tac (Seattle-Tacoma) airport. Here we persuaded a ground mechanic to look the other way while we commandeered a fork-lift truck and, with a large amount of plasticine, made an impression of the Federal Aviation Approved flush mounted non-ramming vent inlet Douglas were using on their DC-9 airliner. Unethical, no doubt, but as the acerbic American scriptwriter Larry David maintains, 'whatever works'. I certainly found this period in big aircraft systems design fascinating.

Meanwhile, things were not going well on the American SST programme. It had been intended that Boeing's 300-seat variable-geometry Model 2707-200 would fly at Mach 2.7. This would have required the extensive use of titanium to withstand skin temperatures at the wing leading edges in excess of 127°C (the point beyond which aluminium begins to lose its strength), which was a factor limiting Concorde's speed to Mach 2.2. The importation

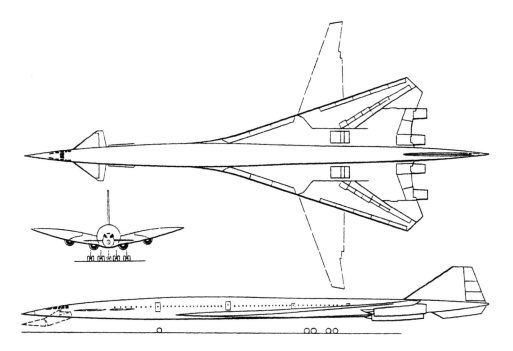

Boeing got as far as displaying a massive full-scale side view of its proposed SST on the side of a hangar facing a main highway. Few could fail to be impressed as they drove by, or by the mock-up showing likely customers, the glamorous interior. It was, however, a step too far and work on the project ceased in 1971. (Boeing Company Publicity)

of titanium sponge from the Soviet Union at a time of international tension, as well as overcoming the machining difficulties associated with this then exotic material, would have created a brand-new set of problems. At the same time, the supersonic design team was facing other major complications concerning reduced range, the reliability of the advanced swing-wing system and an unacceptable increase in structural weight and cost. Despite reverting to Model 2707-300, a smaller, delta-tailed fixed-wing design, not unlike the losing proposal offered by Lockheed in the Federal Aviation Authority's original supersonic design competition, the hurdles proved insurmountable and the Boeing SST programme, unable to overtake or even catch up with Concorde, eventually ground to a halt in 1971.

Americans are eager competitors; or, putting it another way, they take very badly to losing, and to offset this blow to national pride a great deal of industrial effort and money went into supporting the Federal Aviation Authority and the Port Authority of New York in their endeavours to prevent Concorde's entry into the United States. This turned into a long, hard-fought legal battle, the outcome of which is well known enough not to require much elaboration here. Suffice it to say that when finally granted, Concorde's admission to America – where it was not allowed to fly overland at supersonic speeds – could only be regarded as a qualified success.

The 747 mock-up at Boeing's Everett plant. The author is down at the bottom right-hand corner during the buy-off ceremony, a good example of 'Where's Wally'! (Boeing Company Publicity)

If one cannot always look forward with certainty, there is great satisfaction at times in looking back, and American air shows, such as Boeing's Renton Air Festival in July 1967, which featured a restored Boeing Model 247 (which had revolutionised air travel in the mid-1930s), took some beating. It was also at this time that, exposing our daughters to aviation whenever I could, I took Helen up for a flight in a Taylorcraft floatplane belonging to Kurtzer Air Services from Lake Washington. In addition to that interesting experience, both Thelma and I were entranced by Margot Fonteyn and Rudolf Nureyev when, that same evening, they performed in the Royal Ballet's touring production of *Swan Lake* in Seattle's Opera House. It was nice to support the home industries on such a gala occasion.

My time at Boeing fell just short of seeing the first 747 rolled out in September 1968. As much as I wanted to witness this event, there 'ain't no sentiment in business', certainly not American business, and with the need for whatever skills I could offer now having peaked, I was but one of thousands being progressively laid off.

This was a worrying time for Boeing, for although airframes were coming off the production lines, the war in Vietnam had put a priority call on the engines being made at Pratt & Whitney, and it was strange to see so many airliners, with concrete ballast blocks in place of the engines, parked around the plant perimeter. No delivery to the airlines spelled no income for the company and bad news all round. Seattle, its skyline dominated by the impressive Space Needle built in 1962 for the city's World's Fair, was about to become a ghost town. Twenty-aisle supermarkets were whittled down to a single attendant and in 1971, by which time I had moved on, a large banner was stretched across the main highway heading south saying: 'Will the last one to leave Seattle please switch off the light.'

Three years in the 'job-shopping' arena had taught me a thing or two; mainly that, like the meerkat, which is always on the look-out, one had to keep a step ahead where employment

The emergence of the first 747. No doubt a moment for the workers to be proud of, but I had, by then, moved down to join a rival company, McDonnell Douglas in California. (Boeing Company Publicity)

Seattle's endearing feature – the Space Needle. The Sky City restaurant rotates through 360 degrees every forty-seven minutes and affords panoramic views of Puget Sound and the Olympic mountain ranges. It probably affords visitors their first and last impressions of the city.

was concerned. This was not always easy, for the 'old contract hands' knew all the short cuts regarding future employment. But with the Boeing scene quietening down, the recruiting activity at McDonnell Douglas (MDC) in Long Beach and at the Lockheed Aircraft Company in Burbank was gathering pace.

Without a doubt, the Pacific north-west is one of the most beautiful regions in the United States, offering mountains, lakes and forests in abundance, but come late autumn, the six-month period spanning Christmas brings rain, constantly driving in from the ocean. One new arrival on the fuel systems team, Paul Todd, waited but a couple of days before deciding the weather was getting him down and he was going to return to California that night. His wife and children were already fixed up 60 miles away in a rented lodge. Sure enough, I was the one who, after answering the phone the following day, had to explain to his distraught wife, bereft of transport and funds, that 'No, her husband wasn't in the office and that we didn't know his whereabouts'. Halfway through Oregon, we guessed, fast heading south.

8

WELCOME TO THE GOLDEN STATE

After Boeing let me go, the reality of being unemployed for the first time forced me to see things from a different perspective. Standing relatively well dressed in the Seattle dole queue, next to a long line of those less fortunate, proved to be a chastening experience, and it came as quite a shock to realise how suddenly one's circumstances can change. I was lucky, however, for my economic woes were short-lived. Within weeks an offer came through to join a team of General Electric Company designers at McDonnell Douglas in Long Beach, California, then about to install the CF 6 engine in the new DC-10 airliner. Showing true pioneering spirit, it was then a simple matter of organising a quick garage sale of dispensable items, hitching up a U-Haul trailer to transport the domestic essentials, and leaving wet ol' Seattle behind as we headed for sunnier climes.

Taking around four days, the 1,500-mile journey down the Pacific Coast Highway through Oregon via San Francisco to Los Angeles was a truly memorable experience. Memorable not only for picking up my first speeding ticket shortly after entering California, but also for having to drive through 50 miles of fog enshrouding the Big Sur coast road which featured a precipitous drop over the cliff edge on one side. By this time we were adept at adjusting to new surroundings. While many of the Brits, especially the younger unmarried ones, seemed to adapt to the Californian lifestyle almost immediately, we found it to be too transient and lacking substance. One's neighbours always seemed to be on the move, but then so were we. A measure of the fluid relationships there can be gained from the fact that even in the kindergarten class, our girls found themselves to be the only ones living with their true parents. Their young classmates thought this was amazing, and so did we, but for somewhat different reasons.

American aerospace design offices were invariably large and impersonal with no windows to offer distractions. Much like the cities, they were laid out in a large grid with few recognisable landmarks to help you identify where you were. Within half an hour of starting, I found myself disorientated (alright, *lost*) and about to provide the Douglas security people with a good opportunity to show off.

I was supposed to follow the company's in-house rule that required any 'alien' to be accompanied at all times by a permanent employee, even when going to the toilet. I jokingly remarked to one escort that it was going to be a tight squeeze getting both of us into the

General Electric's CF 6 engine, as fitted to the early DC-10 variants, was in the 40,000lb thrust range. Its size may be judged from the one shown here fitted to a B-52A for flight testing. (McDonnell Douglas Archive)

same cubicle, but he was welcome to stay outside and listen if he cared to. 'Don't get smart, buddy' was, I think, the witty gist of his reply. This constraint on movement was, however, not to be taken lightly, and my disregard for it quickly landed me in trouble.

Acting on my own initiative, I wandered down to the CF 6 engine mock-up hall to check some technical details, but found myself being accompanied by an attractive young lady who, considering it was our first date, seemed overly attentive. Warning bells began to ring when I took a wrong turn on the way back to my work station and she suddenly reappeared, telling me that she was the secretarial assistant to the security officer for my area and I shouldn't be unescorted. So what, I thought, but I knew I had overplayed my hand when, shortly after being sheepishly returned to my designated area, a hard-nosed old gal with facial features not unlike the Grand Canyon came striding down the office calling out: 'Cruewdas, any guy called Cruewdas here?' Along with my literally quivering section leader, Joe Barlage, I found myself in a semi-darkened room facing a bright light with an inquisitor, Irving Redwing, barely discernible in the shadows behind. 'Was I aware that I had breached company ordinance number whatever it was' and 'what was my purpose in doing this ...?'

'Guilty as charged, m'lud' was all I could plead and within the hour I was informed by General Electric's manager that I was sacked. Having travelled so far and with a family to get settled in I simply could not believe how ludicrous it was to be fired for doing one's job. I thought it more usual to be 'released' for *not* doing it. With nowhere else to go, I faced the prospect of sitting in the office, *persona non grata*, twiddling my thumbs until the end of the working day. However, it transpired that somewhere along the line my security clearance had got misplaced but was now found. I wasn't judged to be some 'Commie' spy after all. Within a couple of hours I had been hired, fired and rehired, so all was forgiven, but not without some mixed feelings on my part, especially when no apologies were tendered. Was it just me, I wondered, considering my growing propensity for confrontation with US officialdom? Notwithstanding my rehabilitation, I did not find the Douglas design office to be a pleasant working environment and thoughts of returning to England soon began to take root.

Within two weeks of arriving in Los Angeles I was kindly offered another speeding ticket. This time I was the joker trapped in the inside lane between two sets of traffic lights barely 200yd apart, having just exited the company car park. I was not best pleased about that, but I was certainly impressed with the way the Douglas Company handled the fine. A special office inside the plant was dedicated to processing traffic miscreants; when my turn came the administrative assistant quickly placed ticks in the boxes against the number of previous offences, speed over the limit etc. and circled a figure showing the amount to be automatically deducted from my salary – all very efficient and back to work in five minutes. Have a nice day. Next! Considering the long line of fellow employees waiting to be separated from their dollars, I figured that Douglas had a cosy understanding with the local police department and was providing a nice little earner to certain officials not far below the surface.

Soon after this I did have a nice day when, during a weekend wander alongside the Long Beach airfield perimeter track, I spotted – unattended – a vintage Douglas DC-2 airliner. I later found out it belonged to one Colgate W. Darden III, a professor of nuclear physics and an avid collector of vintage aeroplanes. This particular example had made its debut in 1934 and had been flown in for a 1930s-style refurbishment. Keen to get a look inside, I made the usual reconnoitre around the aeroplane to seek permission, but finding no one decided to take an opportunistic approach. Opening the passenger-side door I tried to scramble aboard, but in my haste to be in and out before anyone appeared and asked awkward questions I slipped and gave my shinbone an almighty crack on the door sill. My agonised howl of pain had no effect whatsoever on Helen or Sally, who had accompanied me, as they were far more interested in watching the hundreds of rabbits cavorting about in the long grass alongside the runway. They still laugh about it now!

This DC-2, flown into Long Beach in the late sixties for restoration, had first left the Douglas plant some forty years earlier. (McDonnell Douglas Archive)

The DC-2's cockpit provides an interesting comparison with today's digital flight deck layouts. (McDonnell Douglas Archive)

The DC-8 airliner production line made way for the DC-10 in 1970. Shown here in its final stretched form, this DC-8-73CF displays its aesthetically appealing lines. (McDonnell Douglas Archive)

Design office life in America was, in my experience, far more disciplined than that in a typical British company. On one occasion it was discovered that a worker on the DC-8 production line, with just his legs extending from a fuselage access door, had dropped off to sleep while reading a newspaper. Apart from his instant dismissal, reading material of any kind was immediately prohibited from being brought into the factory, even for lunchtime reading. The one exception to this was the *Wall Street Journal*, which employees were allowed to consult before legitimately calling up their brokers on the east coast at the start of the day. With a three-hour time difference between the east and west coasts, one couldn't afford to slip up on what the New York stock market was doing. I don't consider myself to have a particularly stroppy disposition, but I do find bureaucracy in its extreme form to be vexatious and challenging. So it was in the wake of the reading material embargo. I had struck up a chatty relationship with one of the main entrance security guards, much along the lines of 'Hi Joe, how are you doing?' – 'OK, Limey, you have a nice day now!' But one day he saw the telltale outline of a book I had stuffed into my shirt for lunch-time reading. A minor transgression, I thought, but all pleasantries were quickly dispensed with as he gave me a verbal going over. I like to think it was aimed at impressing his colleagues nearby, but at least I avoided another visit to the dreaded Irving Redwing inquisition room.

The Americans never did anything by halves. One morning a Douglas design engineer, whom I happened to get on with particularly well, was called down to the company's reception area. There, without further ado, he was handcuffed and firmly bundled into the back of a Los Angeles Police Department car. The occupants' white helmets, dark sunglasses and sidearms made this an intimidating experience for my friend, who soon found himself holed up for several hours in the downtown 'holding tank' along with some deeply unsavoury characters. Allowed one phone call only, he managed to get through to his wife who was about to leave the house to sit a university examination; on having to cancel this, she arranged for a lawyer to visit him. In the course of all this, his company security pass was withdrawn pending investigation. And the cause of all this fuss and inconvenience? Some weeks earlier, when driving home with his family from a restaurant, he had been pulled over by a patrolman who advised him that a rear light on his car was not working. He was issued with a caution slip which required him to get the problem fixed within two days. This he did. Unfortunately, his returned slip showing compliance failed to be officially recorded, causing the travelling circuit judge to automatically order his arrest. Though matters were finally put right, I had one very irate American chum fuming at the injustice of it all, insisting that such a thing could never happen in England!

When in 1969 President Nixon cancelled the Manned Orbital Laboratory project, it caused shock waves throughout McDonnell Douglas. Many of the company's technical staff had earlier crossed the big divide separating the aviation and space divisions, and now there was a lemming-like reversal as people tried to look up their previous bosses on the aircraft side. This was not good news for us Brits, as the Southern California Professional Engineers Association immediately clamped down on the use of foreign labour. This was a perfectly understandable attitude and one with which I was in total agreement, and I had actually handed in my notice just before this bombshell arrived (more on that later). Nevertheless, waves of uncertainty were causing widespread unrest among the Long Beach manufacturing workforce, with DC-8 production slowing down to make way for the DC-10.

From late 1968–69, the sales and marketing teams at both the Lockheed Aircraft Company on the other side of town and McDonnell Douglas were fighting fierce campaigns to promote and sell the L1011 TriStar and the DC-10. Further competition in the wide-body field was being provided by Boeing with the 747; and in Europe, Airbus Industries was gaining ground with the introduction of its A300 family of transport aircraft. Things on the civil airliner front were certainly hotting up.

After the first order for thirty General Electric-powered DC-10s was placed by United Airlines, the roll-out of the first machine took place on 23 July 1970 – fifty years and a day since the founding of the Douglas Aircraft Company. This public debut, carried out with much ceremony, beat that of its rival, the TriStar, by just over a month. Though in most respects a successful aeroplane, the DC-10's reputation was forever bruised by two spectacular accidents that caused great loss of life. The first, on 3 March 1974, was the result of explosive decompression near Paris, and the second was due to an engine separating from the wing during take-off from Chicago on 25 May 1979. Though the aircraft's basic design was absolved by the Federal Aviation Administration (FAA) and the National Transport Safety Board (NTSB), these events, alongside a downturn in the world economy, had a major impact on sales.

In 1985 it was announced that, after many refinements and system updates to the basic DC-10 model, board approval had been given to start negotiations with the airlines for what was to be referred to in future as the McDonnell Douglas MD-11. In more recent times, the rollercoaster world of aviation has seen the merger of Boeing and McDonnell Douglas (in 1997), with the aircraft variants now generically referred to as Boeing MD-10s and 11s. Donald Douglas, the founder of the original company, would probably have turned in his grave at the thought of his arch-rival, Bill Boeing, stealing his thunder sixty years later.

Though certainly affording many wonderful sightseeing opportunities, the Californian dream had failed to come up to our family expectations. Living as we did near the Pacific

This was the first artist's impression to be released showing the final choice of engine locations on the DC-10. (McDonnell Douglas Archive)

23 July 1970 saw the first DC-10 roll out at Long Beach, one month ahead of its rival, the Lockheed TriStar. (McDonnell Douglas Archive)

Give me Britain's beaches every time, unless, of course, one happens to be a shareholder in the oil companies. Oil peckers defile the coastline at Huntington Beach. (McDonnell Douglas Archive)

Ocean, one might perhaps conjure up visions of golden sands and a deep-blue sea, but it wasn't like that in Huntington Beach. Around Los Angeles, an ever-widening tide of municipal development seemed to be devouring all in its path. Acres of suburbia laid out on the familiar grid pattern and bounded by endless freeways saw the city edging ever closer to its southerly neighbour, San Diego. While that remains a lasting, somewhat soulless impression, so do the rows of oil peckers down on the beach, relentlessly sucking out the 'black gold'. The smell of oil from the Wilmington refinery pervaded everything in the vicinity. Often, after driving for miles to find air that felt clear and breathable, we discovered that large areas of the beach were privately owned and not accessible to the public. At such times one couldn't help longing for the simple pleasure of walking along the English coast, preferably near Bridlington, unhindered and free, taking in the fresh sea air.

So it came about that in early 1969, having applied for several jobs in the UK, I received an encouraging response from the British Aircraft Corporation (BAC) at Filton near Bristol. The timing worked out well in light of the forthcoming staff reductions at McDonnell Douglas and an interview was arranged to take place at the Disneyland Hotel. Puzzled at the choice of location and unsure of the dress code, I played it safe and wore a formal suit and tie, but couldn't help feeling like a spare part at a wedding as I threaded my way through the crowds of casually dressed holidaymakers. My surprise might then be imagined when I eventually met BAC's representative, Dave Moakes, at a poolside bar clad in Hawaiian shirt and shorts. Though clearly overdressed for the occasion, formalities were soon trimmed to a minimum, and it was in this casual atmosphere, over a couple of beers and a handshake, that I was invited to join the Concorde Powerplant Technical Group. This was a great relief for we could now sail home, safe in the knowledge that another piece in the career jigsaw had been put in place.

9

THE SUPERSONIC DREAM MACHINE

Leaning on the rail of the *Canberra* as she exited San Pedro harbour in Los Angeles, both Thelma and I felt a strong sense of relief at leaving America. Apart from being burgled (by the son of our next-door neighbour), we hadn't experienced any serious traumas, but with the Robert Kennedy and Martin Luther King assassinations fresh in our minds, followed by the Manson murders, the threat of local or national violence never seemed to be far away.

We were immensely glad to be heading home, although after the joy of arrival, integrating ourselves back into the British way of life did bring certain difficulties. Not the least of these involved adjusting to the interminable industrial strikes and those connected with the girls' new schooling. From an early age, all American kids become part of the 'show and tell'

Robert and Ethel Kennedy celebrate his winning the 1968 California primary election. Minutes later he was shot and lay dying in the Ambassador hotel. His assassination took place just prior to our leaving America. (*Robert Francis Kennedy Memorial Issue*)

Drawing boards aplenty at BAC Filton and loftsmen at work in Toulouse, as Concorde design work progresses in the sixties. Spline curves and lead weights are still in evidence, as indeed they were during my period in Fairey's lofting department. (Bristol Archive)

culture. This had required Helen and Sally, along with their classmates, to stand up each Monday morning and talk about their weekend experiences; but once back in England, and by then aged 7 and 5, their confident vocal abilities failed to offset their written work which was said to be below the necessary standard. Though keen to do well, their outgoing 'Californian' style of behaviour was perceived by some to be 'pushy' and not viewed favourably by those teachers of a more conservative disposition. Following a move to Hambrook Primary School near Winterbourne, it wasn't long before both Helen and Sally had become more settled and in tune with the local schooling system.

I joined the Concorde Powerplant Technical Group in late 1969 and soon realised that it worked alongside some of the best aerodynamicists, designers and engineers within the industry. My formal duties as propulsion project engineer were to co-ordinate the technical aspects of the Olympus engine intake and exhaust installations, along with other aircraft system interfaces. What this entailed in practice was to ensure good communication between the engine manufacturer, Rolls-Royce, the French SNECMA company charged with the design of the reheat system, and the British Aircraft Corporation, itself responsible for, among other key work packages, the engine air intake and the clamshell-type reverse thrust

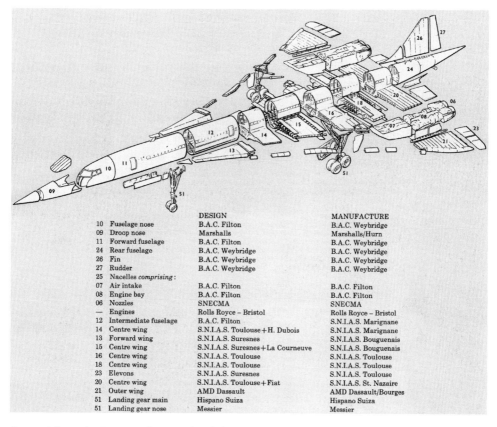

		DESIGN	MANUFACTURE
10	Fuselage nose	B.A.C. Filton	B.A.C. Weybridge
09	Droop nose	Marshalls	Marshalls/Hurn
11	Forward fuselage	B.A.C. Filton	B.A.C. Weybridge
24	Rear fuselage	B.A.C. Weybridge	B.A.C. Weybridge
26	Fin	B.A.C. Weybridge	B.A.C. Weybridge
27	Rudder	B.A.C. Weybridge	B.A.C. Weybridge
25	Nacelles *comprising*:		
07	Air intake	B.A.C. Filton	B.A.C. Filton
08	Engine bay	B.A.C. Filton	B.A.C. Filton
06	Nozzles	SNECMA	SNECMA
—	Engines	Rolls Royce – Bristol	Rolls Royce – Bristol
12	Intermediate fuselage	B.A.C. Filton	S.N.I.A.S. Marignane
14	Centre wing	S.N.I.A.S. Toulouse+H. Dubois	S.N.I.A.S. Marignane
13	Forward wing	S.N.I.A.S. Suresnes	S.N.I.A.S. Bouguenais
15	Centre wing	S.N.I.A.S. Suresnes+La Courneuve	S.N.I.A.S. Bouguenais
16	Centre wing	S.N.I.A.S. Toulouse	S.N.I.A.S. Toulouse
18	Centre wing	S.N.I.A.S. Toulouse	S.N.I.A.S. Toulouse
23	Elevons	S.N.I.A.S. Suresnes	S.N.I.A.S. Toulouse
20	Centre wing	S.N.I.A.S. Toulouse+Fiat	S.N.I.A.S. St. Nazaire
21	Outer wing	AMD Dassault	AMD Dassault/Bourges
51	Landing gear main	Hispano Suiza	Hispano Suiza
51	Landing gear nose	Messier	Messier

Concorde's production manufacturing breakdown. (Bristol Archive)

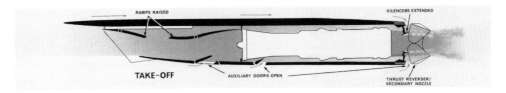

Powerplant configurations for take-off and supersonic cruise. (Bristol Archive)

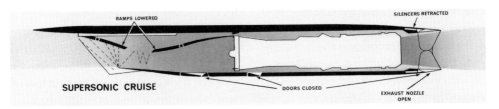

My boss, Ted Talbot, carried great responsibility for Concorde's intake design. (Ted Talbot)

systems. As might be imagined, such integration was a moving feast on many technical and political levels and this basic job description hardly begins to encompass the total manpower required. Still, one did one's best.

To make such a simple reference to the engine air intake fails to convey what a complicated and brilliant engineering achievement it was. Required to decelerate the air entering it from 1,350mph (Mach 2) to 350mph over a duct distance of some 13ft before it entered the engine's axial compressor, involved a system of extremely fast-acting ramps controlled by digital computers, themselves in their infancy. The ramps, reacting to sensors within the intake ducting, generated a series of shock waves, which, acting as barriers, slowed the air down sufficiently for it to be comfortably digested by the engine.

A significant part of the powerplant test programme was in establishing the engine surge envelope, i.e. the altitude and speed conditions beyond which the engine makes decidedly nasty banging noises and refuses to play nicely. The whole intake system had to react instantly and reliably over a wide range of environmental and potential failure conditions which, just for good measure, could not be allowed to adversely affect the adjacent engine. Though development problems naturally occurred, all the airworthiness targets, many of which were formulated as the programme evolved, were satisfactorily met. Needless to say, it was a matter of great pride that the team achieved what the Americans and Russians notably failed to do.

Concorde's highly innovative intake system was once famously described by the aeroplane's chief designer, Sir Archibald Russell, as 'the second most complicated inlet known to man'. Pause for a smile. However, if God ever senses that man is catching up, I wager that He will think up something smarter to re-establish his position as inventor-in-chief.

I find it amazing that the Russian TU-144 'Concordski' achieved what it did, with its engines relying not on 'fly-by-wire' inputs like Concorde, but on straight-through mechanical linkages which probably generated excessive amounts of noise and vibration. How the intake would have responded to gust conditions at Mach 2 defies belief. Impressions remain of a visit to Filton by a Russian design delegation, when one member pulled out a spring-loaded metal tape and measured the dimensions of Concorde's intake!

NASA engineers, too, were in awe of Ted Talbot when he later visited various research establishments in the US – he was the assistant chief propulsion engineer regarded as a leading international expert on supersonic intake design. He would describe how it was possible for 'a hundred old dears, crossing the Atlantic at three miles a second, to delicately sip their champagne with never a space suit in sight'. Given the chance to fly in Concorde with a British test crew, hardened American pilots were amazed at the aircraft's docility when first one, then two engines were chopped at Mach 2 to simulate a double failure. Flying 'hands off' for several seconds before resuming control, BAC's pilots demonstrated that Concorde showed no inclination to misbehave at all during such extreme conditions.

It would be difficult to imagine a more impressive sight, or sound, than that of Concorde taking off. The noise generated on a typically thunderous departure was truly earth-shaking

Russia's TU-144 'Concordski' made its maiden flight and reached Mach 1 and Mach 2 slightly ahead of Concorde, but it would never have met international airworthiness requirements. (*The Concorde Story*, 1986)

Left: Possessing the power of a beast, and the grace of a lady, Britain's Concorde 002 lands at Fairford, following its maiden flight on 9 April 1969. (Bristol Archive)

Below: A first-day cover commemorating Concorde's achieving Mach 2 on 12 November 1970. (Bristol Archive)

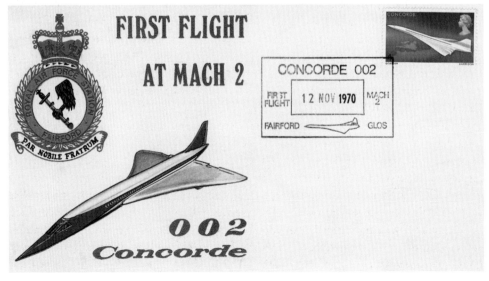

and though great efforts were made to introduce various types of silencing equipment, total success proved elusive. This was largely due to the inherently noisy turbojet being the engine of choice in the 1950s, when excessive loudness, though obviously unwelcome, was regarded as an inevitable by-product of higher speed. By the 1970s, however, pressure groups were not only relentlessly campaigning against the aircraft's take-off noise, but also the unknown effects of its sonic booms on people and property on the ground, and the amount of nitrous oxide exhaust gases that would enter the upper atmosphere. With the initial prospect of hundreds of supersonic aircraft polluting the airways, they certainly had a case. Faced with these concerns, Concorde's top-level management, assisted by expert legal and scientific representation, had to fight constant technical, political and environmental battles to defend the project.

At the outset of the struggle for supersonic supremacy between the European and American design teams, it was generally considered that 'speed would always sell'. However, by 1972 the aviation landscape had changed considerably. Not only had the cost of fuel risen dramatically, but the arrival of the subsonic Boeing 747 had introduced the 'bigger but slower' option into the airlines' cost equations. Despite the initial optimism surrounding the first orders for seventy-four Concordes, when Pan American World Airways cancelled its order in 1973, the sixteen other airline customers, no longer faced with having to re-equip their fleets with expensive supersonic machines to remain competitive, very quickly and with undisguised relief followed suit. This left just British Airways and Air France, both heavily subsidised by their governments, to operate a total of seven aircraft each out of the twenty eventually built.

The first difficulties experienced by the British and French companies regarding design configuration and work share were soon resolved, but the British government's reluctance to continue the project in the light of escalating costs put a constant strain on relations with its Gallic partners. Collaboration with the French was thought by the British government to be a persuasive tool in gaining entry into the European Common Market, but General de Gaulle, still resentful of wartime snubs by Prime Minister Winston Churchill and the American President Franklin Roosevelt, continued to stonewall Britain's admission.

It is a source of wonderment to me still that Concorde ever saw the light of day, not least because of that just described, but also considering the general British disregard for and (certainly in my case) total ineptitude for foreign languages. Twice weekly classes in French at Filton Technical College, starting at 7.30 a.m., were not received with great enthusiasm by the technical workforce, and it was quite common for us not to turn up due to meetings in Toulouse or Paris. Technical meetings with the French, whose command of the English language was infinitely better than our understanding of theirs, could be fraught affairs, especially when controversial issues had to be discussed. It was soon realised that when in France, our counterparts employed a cunning strategy for getting their own way. Faced with an impasse, the French chairman would suggest that more time be given to the problem and that talks should be continued in the afternoon. Lunch, being a convivial affair, saw an occasional lowering of the British guard, but not that of our hosts who, by continually topping up the Brits' wine glasses, relied on the seductive power of the grape and much bonhomie to weaken our stance.

On one famous occasion, a successful counter-attack was cleverly carried out. The French were challenged to a competition in which teams were blindfolded and each member asked to guess whether the wine they were drinking was red or white. What kind of idiot, one may ask, would suggest such a contest on the opposition's home ground? But determined not to be outdone, the Brits had a fiendish trick up their sleeves. The French hosts were invited to go first and though naturally doing well, there came a point when one of their lads made an incorrect call. It became apparent now that we had sufficient 'runs in the bag' to win. Our opponents, however, had been set up, for earlier it had been noted that the bar used two sets of virtually identical wine glasses. The tray prepared for the British team by its 'non-playing' captain contained a mix of glasses: those with a certain shape of stem held white wine, the remainder held red. Though blindfolded, the variation in the stem shape was discernible to the touch and allowed the well-briefed and relatively sober BAC team to record a historic 100 per cent victory – away from home, as well! Perfidious Albion, you may cry, but with international prestige at stake, one couldn't take unnecessary risks. One only has to look at the bribing process allegedly employed by countries wishing to host football's next World Cup, or a certain Middle Eastern state allegedly paying an extraordinary amount of cash to guarantee a couple of gold medals at 2012's Olympic boxing events. No messing about there, simply a question of political priorities taking precedence over moral values.

Engineers are, by their calling, pragmatic individuals not given to dithering indecision. One such veteran practitioner was Eric Hyde, BAC's special projects director, whose high-level responsibilities included the Concorde powerplant. Every morning at 9 a.m. the main departmental heads assembled in his office for 'morning prayers'; that is, most of the attendees prayed for deliverance from Eric's caustic tongue. Not many escaped. My role was to set the general scene by recounting the previous day's happenings. Though always eventful, these were difficult to round up and summarise in the limited time between arriving in the office at 8.30 and the start of the meeting. The flight test programme reports from Fairford and Toulouse, followed by an outline of the technical problems being encountered 'down the hill' at Rolls-Royce's Patchway factory, were usually enough to make Eric less than pleased and all too often incandescent with rage. Three areas of conversation were always avoided. Firstly, Weybridge and the Vickers contingent at Filton; secondly, the Royal Navy, whose wartime gunners had an avowed intention to shoot down anything that flew (including him as a Second World War pilot); thirdly, Rolls-Royce which, though clearly faced with difficulties of their own with the Olympus engine, were in his view entirely undeserving of understanding and wholly responsible for holding up BAC's progress. With such outsized chips on both shoulders, one couldn't accuse Eric of not having a balanced view.

It was a Rolls-Royce issue that caused him to despatch me to Madrid at a couple of hours' notice. Armed with a Special Flying Instruction, my mission was to warn the pilots already carrying out 'hot and high' trials to avoid dwelling at a certain compressor rpm as the engines were spooled up for take-off. Failure to observe this would, it was predicted, produce catastrophic vibration within seconds. Arriving in the late evening, I discovered that no one spoke English, not even on the British Airways reception desk. I had imagined that after disembarking from my flight I would soon see the big white bird parked within easy reach, but my enquiries as to its whereabouts seemed only to cause amusement. Eventually I found a taxi driver who pointed out that Concorde wasn't at Madrid's main airport but at Torrejón, a US Air Force base some 20 miles away. Sure enough, when I finally arrived I saw with relief the familiar shape on the far side of the airfield. The airman on guard duty arranged for Jeep transport to take me over, but pointed out that I would have to wait some time for it. By the time it turned up and delivered me to the aeroplane, I was alone under the apron floodlights – except for one nightwatchman, fortunately British, who informed me that all the other ground and flight crew had returned to their hotel in Madrid. This was not what I wanted to hear and my patience was wearing decidedly thin. I required yet another lift back to the main gate and a further taxi ride, this time to the hotel, where I finally met up with the aircrew in the bar in what I would describe as a very relaxed state. So relaxed were they that no one wanted to listen to my message saying it could wait until the following morning's technical briefing. I thought that to be a particularly good idea and soon became rather relaxed myself.

My Spanish venture provided a unique opportunity to ride in the 'dickey' seat, just behind the pilot, on a rejected take-off trial. The aim of this test was to determine tyre and brake pad temperatures after an acceleration to lift-off speed followed by an immediate closing of the throttles and the application of reverse thrust. With Concorde's crew compartment overhanging the nose wheels by 11m, this manoeuvre induced a mighty pitch-down attitude and it would not have been a good idea to leave one's restraining straps unfastened. I had secretly hoped that the race down the runway would miraculously transform into a flight, but it was to be another couple of years before the eventful day came when I became entitled to wear the esteemed Mach 2 tie.

With the instructions dutifully passed on to the aircrew, I chanced to enter a nearby hangar where the Spanish Air Force kept a number of outdated CASA 2-111 bombers. These were licence-built versions of the German Heinkel 111 of Second World War fame, which, powered by Rolls-Royce Merlin engines, had been used in the 1969 film *The Battle of Britain*. Here was a chance not to be missed so, with no one in evidence, I climbed aboard one that had its entry door conveniently open and, sitting in the pilot's seat, enjoyed a thoroughly Walter Mitty moment.

The magnificent all-round view afforded by the fully glazed cockpit was, I thought, seriously offset by the lack of crew protection and it must have been a chilling experience to

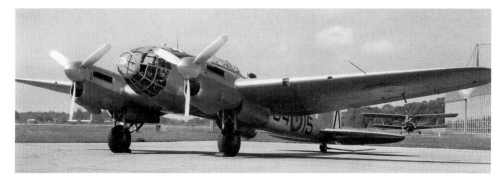

A CASA 2-111 of the Spanish Air Force shows off its high-visibility flight deck.

be faced with a frontal fighter attack in battle. Dreaming away, I wasn't aware of the Spanish Air Force sergeant behind me until he tapped me on the shoulder and asked if he could be allowed on board Concorde since I had visited his aeroplane. Although a fair enough request, I knew it would be tricky to accomplish, and after briefly discussing his request with Concorde's ground crew chief, I had to tell him that regrettably it wasn't possible as the aircraft was in the final stages of being prepared for flight. At least, that was the diplomatic version of the crew chief's two-word epithet.

The trials personnel were not always so abrupt and could be downright charming when it suited, as witnessed one evening when a dozen or so of us were seated in an open-air restaurant, nattering on about the day's happenings. No one had noticed the solitary American sitting at an adjacent table who was clearly tuned in to our general conversation. At last he could contain himself no longer and, keen to ingratiate himself, announced his willingness to fund the entire meal if he could join the party. Suddenly, charm was the order of the day, and after making known our intention to move on to a Flamenco bar, he insisted that it would be his privilege to pay for the whole evening. To the BAC employees, always hard-pressed to explain away their expense claims, it seemed as if Santa Claus had put in a welcome guest appearance. However, I reckon our benefactor probably got his money's worth from telling the folks back home how he had been invited to join the Concorde crowd for an evening out.

From the foregoing, one might gather that Eric Hyde was not inclined to sympathetic understanding. In fairness, he was but one of many hard-driving individuals I came across in my long years in aviation. Such men, constantly pitted against one another, had to be extremely determined in making sure their views were heeded and, most importantly, acted upon. Yet mindful of this, leaving Eric's office usually offered the kind of relief one felt after a particularly gruelling session at the dentist.

Many words have already been used to describe the political and technical complexities that attended Concorde, and it is not my intention to dwell much more on the now-long-dead pros and cons debate. But it is perhaps of interest to recall the intensity of feeling this beautiful but controversial lady aroused both within and without the industry. Was Concorde the iconic national flag-bearer that we minions at BAC were conditioned to believe it was, or was it a cuckoo in the nest that continued to demand ever-increasing amounts of public money, which arguably denied funding for other, less glamorous projects? One thing is certain: when supersonic transport began to be seriously considered in the early 1960s, Europe's aircraft industry was facing a bleak future and was about to be totally eclipsed by the big players in America. The previous decade had seen Britain's bright start with the beautiful jet-powered Comet come to grief following the loss of several machines in service. These disasters had enabled Boeing, though shedding crocodile tears at de Havilland's terrible misfortune, and aided by a vast funding spin-off from the company's KC-135 air refuelling tanker, to confidently develop the highly successful 707 civil airliner. As is well known, this aircraft went on to monopolise the world's subsonic jet market. Forget 'level playing fields' and where we in Britain *would* have been if only the Comet had maintained its early lead. American entrenchment in the jet transport business was almost at the point where it could never be challenged. It had seemed that the only way forward for Europe's designers was to leap-frog the subsonic market and establish a lead in supersonic design and manufacture – which is more or less where this chapter began.

The time I spent at Filton, from 1969 to 1975, coincided with the most intensive period of Concorde's design, development and flight test activity. But inevitably, as the company's efforts began to focus more on production, many employees on the design side began to view the future with concern. As described in the earlier chapters, situations similar to this had

Telegrams: Britair Bristol Telex   Telex 44163

British Aircraft Corporation Limited

COMMERCIAL AIRCRAFT DIVISION

G.P.O. BOX No. 77

Your Ref:

FILTON HOUSE - BRISTOL BS 99 7AR

Our Ref: JET/EMO   TELEPHONE BRISTOL 693831   *Ext.* 184

5th May, 1975

South African Embassy,
Trafalgar Square,
London.

To Whom It May Concern

Dear Sir,

   This letter confirms that Mr. Colin Cruddas has been continually employed at the British Aircraft Corporation, Filton, England, from September 1969.

   During this period Mr. Cruddas attained management status, initially as Deputy Head of the Concorde Powerplant Technical Group, before becoming Propulsion Project Engineer in 1972.

   His duties have been principally concerned with co-ordinating all the technical aspects of the Olympus power-plant including the intake and exhaust installation with associated aircraft system interfaces, for eventual certificatic These responsibilities have entailed extensive liaison with the associated engine and airframe companies along with the Airworthiness Authorities.

   In the Companies estimation, the way in which Mr. Cruddas has performed the above duties has made a very significant contribution towards the achievement of C. of A. for the Concorde powerplant. Consequently, his presence will be sorely missed.

   Yours faithfully,

J.E. Talbot
Asst. Chief Propulsion Engineer

BAC's kind recommendation, courtesy of Ted Talbot, no doubt assisted my Atlas Aircraft appointment.

precipitated the need to get on one's bike and seek other employment, as Norman Tebbit had colourfully described it. And so, with no Concorde Mark II in the offing, the possibility of a move away from Bristol was, by early 1975, turning into a necessity. But where to and to do what proved difficult questions. The answer came, as so often happens, as a result of several coincident events.

One Sunday evening, Thelma, myself and the girls were watching a TV programme hosted by the South African naturalist Laurens van der Post, which showed the wildlife likely to be seen on a typical safari. It looked incredibly captivating and enticing, especially when compared to the dreariness of the British winter we were then experiencing. The following morning I had occasion to go into Ted Talbot's office, but had to wait as he was engaged in a telephone conversation with his back to me. It was then that I noticed on his desk an open magazine with the words 'Engineers Required for South Africa' standing out in bold type. Ted's phone call was prolonged enough for me to read, albeit upside down, that anyone interested should call South Africa House in Trafalgar Square for an interview. Time, however, was at a premium, for the interviewing team was due to return home within the next few days; this required a major decision that could not be taken without much consideration. Having spent five years gutting and restoring what we now called Rose Cottage, Thelma was naturally reluctant to consider another overseas move. Her reaction was also influenced by having worked in the Afrikaans news section at the BBC, which had not proved to be an enlightening experience. Nevertheless, when faced with the threat of possible unemployment, the lure of an African adventure provided an alternative that was hard to resist. It appeared even more attractive when, after the interview (which we all attended), I was immediately offered the position of chief designer (systems) at the Atlas Aircraft Company located near Johannesburg. Needless to say, both our girls needed little persuasion; they were already envisioning wild animals queuing up to be fed outside the front door.

After getting off to such a quick-fire start, it took almost a year to complete the sale of our house and sort out the continuous stream of bureaucratic paperwork emanating from the South African government. There was also the further complication of the girls having adopted, or should I say purposely enticed, a cat from a nearby farm into their care, and part of the family emigration deal was that the cat went with us. 'If the cat doesn't go, we don't go' was the ultimatum put on the table by our two budding Trade Union officials. Clearly they had been seeing too much of Arthur Scargill who never seemed to be off the TV screen.

Family separations are never easy and, after a poignant Christmas spent with our parents in Bridlington, it was in a rented minibus that the four of us, plus Pushkin the cat and twenty-odd assorted cases and bags, drove down to London and caught the train to Southampton's docks. Our last seagoing venture had seen us joyously returning home on the *Canberra* to these same docks. Now, on 22 January 1976, we faced a more subdued departure on the Safmarine Line's *Vaal* heading for Cape Town, exactly ten years to the day that we left England by air for work in Seattle.

10

NEEDED BUT NOT WANTED

When returning home from America on the *Canberra*, Thelma – by her own admission not the best sailor in the world – had seen little of the western Atlantic. This is not surprising considering her movement had been restricted to the short distance between bed and toilet bowl. Her discomfort on that occasion was exceeded on the *Vaal*, and she spent three days in acute cabin confinement. Our girls, too, were similarly afflicted as we pitched and rolled through the Bay of Biscay. It was only after anti-sickness injections by the ship's doctor that my womenfolk slowly slumbered their way to recovery. I, meanwhile, having also suffered but to a lesser degree, valiantly made my way a couple of times to the dining room, only to find it virtually deserted, with but few other hardy shipmates willing to face food. Fortunately, life returned to normal soon afterwards and we settled down to enjoy the shipboard activities and the increasing warmth of the sun as we steamed towards the equator. When the ship was off Dakar on the West African coast, I heard in the sky an all-too-familiar sound, and sure enough, there was an Air France Concorde winging its way across our path en route to Rio de Janeiro. I don't recall any Americans being present on the *Vaal* which was unfortunate, because the chance to point out their country's inability to produce a comparable machine would have made my day. Evoking memories of Madrid, I might even have coerced one to host dinner that evening, but it was not to be. Eighteen days after leaving England, I climbed up on deck in the early dawn light to get a first glimpse of Table Mountain on the horizon. It all looked very exciting as we steamed into Cape Town, but I'm not sure what our cat, still ensconced in its deck kennel, made of its new surroundings.

We had made friends on board the *Vaal* with a South African family, who gave us a broad insight into what life in a society divided by apartheid held in store. I should add that during our family interview at South Africa House, this emotive political issue had been smoothly glossed over by an experienced team. They had described apartheid as a case of 'separate development' which was working well, but at that time I simply hadn't known the right questions to ask.

Our arrival in Cape Town brought us face to face with the realities of this disarming euphemism. In true tourist style, we innocently wandered into a restaurant only for it to be firmly pointed out that it was a 'blacks only' area and we had to leave. Naively we said that we didn't mind staying, but the native staff, whose agitation was evident, didn't know what to make of white folk taking this strange attitude and we were gently encouraged to make a quick but bemused exit.

Later, we were taken up the long winding road to the base of Table Mountain by our new friends, who then left us to our own devices. After taking the cable car to the top, it was a joy to soak in the magnificent views and marvel at the sight of the city spread out so

Once through the Bay of Biscay, life on board the SA *Vaal* became a highly pleasurable experience. Here the ship departs from Cape Town. (SAF Marine Publicity)

The walk down, in the dark, from the base of Cape Town's Table Mountain was a formidable ordeal.
A massive misjudgement on my part.

far below. Dusk began to fall and on exiting the cable car we were alarmed to find that all
of the fast-disappearing taxis had been pre-booked and there was no other form of public
transport. Suddenly, with no one else in sight, it looked a long walk back through areas
that were considered highly dangerous for white people to be in, even during the day. Faced
with no alternative, however, we set off down what had become a dark and very uncertain
road. After half an hour or so, the lights of Cape Town seemed little nearer and I became
increasingly concerned for our safety. Eventually we found ourselves in one of the townships
on the city outskirts and not knowing what else to do we went into the first shop we saw.
The Portuguese owner insisted that we stayed in the shop until he had arranged for a taxi
to take us back to the city. All ended well, but back in the safety of the Tulbagh Hotel we
realised that we had been lucky to avoid serious trouble and that life in South Africa was
completely different from anything we had previously experienced.

Racial differentiation was further reinforced the next day when we boarded the famed Blue Train for the 926-mile journey to Johannesburg. There are trains, and there are *trains*, and this one bore little resemblance to the 8.20 from Waterloo. Running on rubber-coated wheels at no more than 50mph, the Blue Train simply glided along with only two or three stops along the way until it reached Johannesburg twenty-six hours later. Without wanting this to read like a travel brochure, it would be hard to fault the luxurious fittings that included gold-tinted windows to reduce the glare from the African sun and magnificent floral displays in the restaurant car. This was an experience clearly intended for whites only.

Atlas had arranged for us to stay in a block of transit flats in Kempton Park until we took possession of the house provided by the company. Our first night in this temporary accommodation proved traumatic. Invited to the home of my future boss, Norman Barraud, for dinner, we returned to find our cat, which had travelled all this distance in a wicker basket and special deck kennel, had gone missing. Somehow, she had answered freedom's call and taken off through a small window. Although it was raining 'cats and dogs', unfortunately our cat wasn't one of them! Africa's rain and electrical storms are something truly special, as we found out while trying to find our errant pet. Wandering up and down the surrounding, unfamiliar streets calling 'Pushkin' felt rather ridiculous, but our gloom could not have been deeper as we stood amidst our unpacked cases. We put an advertisement in the local paper, but as we were informed by the other transit flat residents, 'poor thing, most likely down a snake's throat or in an African cooking pot by now'. This was not the news I wanted to leave with the girls as I headed off for Atlas the next day. But after a week, to our amazement, someone asked me if our cat was a Persian and pointed to a fur bundle lying outside his flat. How she had survived we shall never know, but survive she did, and with this source of depression lifted, we felt much more at one with the world.

Our newfound well-being soon evaporated, however, when we were driven by the company's 'Mr Fixit', Marnie Englebrecht, to see the rent-free house that formed part of my remuneration package. We were genuinely speechless after pulling up outside a single-storey building to see a large group of Africans sitting outside the gate stirring the contents of a cooking pot. What, or dare I say who, was in it we did not wish to find out and my first reaction was to drive back to the company and demand to know what on earth was going on. Having 'burned one's boats' in coming this far, we just had to make the best of the situation. Faced with this disappointment Thelma, having had the strongest reservations about leaving Rose Cottage, demonstrated her stoic qualities and it didn't take me long to call on mine when I actually started work at the company.

The only way forward was to forget the promised inducement, buy our own house and for me to align myself with the Atlas regime which, being politically driven, was unlike anything I was used to. All the people at design management level were British ex-pats, but those in senior executive positions were, almost without exception, of Afrikaner descent. Atlas had been formed in 1965 to provide a degree of manufacturing independence following the United Nations' arms embargo imposed two years earlier. It was essentially an offshoot of Armscor which, located in Pretoria and much like the British Ministry of Defence, influenced defence policy and controlled the procurement of military equipment. The South African Air Force (SAAF) relied heavily on its imported fleet of French Mirage III fighter-bombers and

The Aermacchi MB 326 was built in South Africa under licence as the Impala. It convinced me that high-performance aerobatics was something best left to the professionals. (Atlas Archive)

the Italian Aermacchi MB.326 (built by Atlas under licence as the Impala) for training and ground attack aircraft. Having expressed my wish to fly in an Impala, Atlas's amiable chief test pilot, Wing Commander Newton Harrison, arranged for me to 'go along for the ride' one bright morning.

'Wingco' asked in a deceptively disarming way if I 'fancied doing a bit'. 'Sure,' I replied. 'That's fine by me!' A cloudless day over Jo'burg, an expert pilot and a highly responsive aircraft – what more could one want? Aerobatics, however, are an acquired taste and I've long since realised that they are not compatible with my constitution. After a succession of increasingly high g-turns, followed by tail slides with a quick wing-over and a near vertical dive, the ejector seat offered a tempting means of early release. But despite holding on until, with canopy slid fully back, we finally touched down, to my shame breakfast reappeared as we taxied slowly in – just when I thought I had got away with it and could have said, with mild conviction, that I had really enjoyed the flight. Better luck next time, perhaps, but in the meantime it was back to the drawing board.

Repair schemes and modifications to the imported types kept the design office fully stretched. Even so, it was necessary for any work to be submitted to the respective parent companies in France and Italy for final approval. Atlas, nevertheless, laid claim to having designed the C.4 Kudu, which in truth was a direct copy of Aermacchi's AM.3 Bosbok (Bush

The Atlas C.4 'Kudu', was South Africa's first attempt at an indigenously designed aircraft. It was, nevertheless, closely based on the Aermacchi 'Bosbok'. (Atlas Archive)

Buck) single-engined light transport. Though the military prototype had been flying for six months or so before I arrived at Atlas, it was still prone to engine exhaust fumes entering the enclosed cabin and this proved to be a difficult problem to cure.

Forty of these machines were eventually delivered to the SAAF which, in addition to a sizeable number of Harvard trainers and Dakota transports, also employed several other types, notably the Avro Shackleton for coastal and ocean patrol and the Buccaneer for counter-insurgency operations. Strangely, in my four years at Atlas I don't recall either of these British imports calling for any major work to be done by Atlas on the design side. There was, however, no shortage of high-flying ideas that floated down from the company board level for the half a dozen British group leaders to consider. It was asked, for example, what would be required in the way of manpower and facilities to (a) re-spar the Shackleton; (b) look at a Buccaneer replacement; or (c) design a helicopter? Answers on a postcard please by the end of the week. With absolutely no access to basic design criteria or experienced personnel willing to come from overseas (I was almost the last to do so at that time), the task of making credible assessments regarding the various types of skills required and the number of people needed was virtually hopeless. Having presented our pessimistic, yet practical views to our politically appointed executive management, the rejoinder came back that we would be expected to train sufficient graduates leaving the South African universities. Such training would have to be done in addition to carrying out our routine duties. Norman Barraud, though South African, had at one time worked at de Havilland in the UK and could well understand the difficulties we faced; and I know he had a torrid time trying to convince those who ran the company that we were being realistic and not deliberately obstructive.

Following the placement of a recruitment advertisement in the press, myself and Mac McLintic, an ex-de Havilland man running the structures group, flew down to Cape Town to interview all *four* prospective applicants. I was keen to recruit someone who was familiar with installing radio equipment in aircraft. The only respondent was a trawler deckhand who said he was used to switching on his fishing boat's Decca radar set. His admirable qualification fell somewhat short of what I had in mind. Another man, keen to show off his drawing skills, brought along a large three-view illustration he had made of a submarine. Half of it was drawn in pencil, largely unsharpened by the look of it, and the rest of it in ink.

The supply of Buccaneers to South Africa proved a serious problem for Harold Wilson's government. This picture shows a rocket-assisted take-off at RAF Elvington, but surprisingly this facility was rarely used by the South African Air Force. (Blackburn Archive)

Solving the problem of corrosion of the Lockheed L1011 undercarriage retraction system proved to be a thorny problem for the Atlas Design Group. (Mike Phipp Collection)

In a world of choice we could probably have acted like theatrical impresarios selecting girls for a chorus line, but Mac and I were seriously stretched in finding anyone who was either experienced or even trainable. None of those we interviewed fell even remotely into either category. This shortage of skills meant we had to do a good deal of 'reverse engineering' in order to keep machines flying. Whereas in normal situations the most expedient repair would entail getting a replacement component from the original manufacturer, it was now essential that such items be manufactured 'in-house'. This was often far from easy to do. By simply holding the component to be reproduced in one's hand, we had to guess the grade of various materials, what treatments had been applied, whether the item was on top or bottom limits and if it had been the subject of a works query or design concession procedures etc. Any reader having a technical understanding might appreciate the problems involved when the 8ft-long screw jacks and ball nuts forming part of the Lockheed L1011 undercarriage retraction mechanism were found to have severe pitting corrosion. The aircraft were operated by Safair at Cape Town, where the salty air was said to have caused the problem. Approaches to Lockheed in the US brought no worthwhile response and it was only after finding a factory in Switzerland with a machine bed long enough to accommodate the jacks, that the skimming of the threads could take place and a repair scheme put in hand.

The meeting of essential manpower needs remained a serious problem throughout my period at Atlas. Not only did future recruiting cause much head-scratching, but coming

Aeronautical Society of South Africa
Lugvaartkundige Vereniging van Suid-Afrika

GRAND FINAL

AEROMASTER TEAM OF TRANSVAAL – 1977

PROGRAMME

Jumbo Room – Holiday Inn – Jan Smuts Airport

Saturday November 26th

023

The Aeromaster Team competition brought together all the major aviation organisations in the Transvaal.

to terms with one or two of the British ex-pats in the design office, who regarded me as an unwelcome intruder, required special attention. One, who greeted my introduction with 'So you're the new arrival, are you?', had previously worked at Gloster Aircraft and eccentrically timed his movements in and out of the office with an old-fashioned alarm clock. Another, an Irish ex-RAF sergeant, was technically very proficient, but having, shall we say, a wedded addiction to alcohol he tended to turn up for work on an irregular basis. On more than one occasion it was necessary for me to drive round to his apartment and bang on the door, FBI-style, demanding that he 'open up'. One time, when he opened the door minus any vestige of clothing, he observed: 'Oh God, it's Jasus [sic] Christ himself.' Praise indeed, but I had a problem that needed his earthly attention, so I simply had to wait in the car until he eventually made a clothed and relatively sober appearance. Being Irish he could, if so inclined, charm the monkeys out of the trees, but he certainly caused me a headache or two.

In the 1980s, by which time I had left the firm, circumstances changed considerably and using technology from the licence-built Aérospatiale Super Puma, Denel Aviation, having absorbed Atlas, produced the country's first indigenously designed helicopter, the Rooivalk (Red Kestrel). This was certainly no mean achievement, though gained with considerable assistance from the French. A pool of technical expertise was thus finally formed but the Rooivalk was only delivered in small numbers to the SAAF and no export orders have yet been received. Damned in certain quarters as over-sophisticated, overpriced, over-delayed and out of date (did I miss anything?), it seems well qualified to take its place alongside a number of aircraft that suffered a similar fate in Britain.

Outside of factory life, I was especially pleased to initiate and organise an aeronautical 'mastermind' quiz competition, in conjunction with ex-Folland Aircraft aerodynamicist Malcolm Tait and other colleagues in the company. Taking part were several teams from within the Transvaal that included the Johannesburg Light Aeroplane Club, the South African Air Force, the Experimental Aircraft Association, the Royal Aeronautical Society (Aeronautical Society of South Africa) and Atlas itself; the prize was a beautiful silver Spitfire trophy donated by a local businessman, Larry Barnett. Having gone to great lengths to set this up, the effort required to sustain it as an ongoing event proved too much and to my regret the competition lapsed after I returned to England in 1979.

Like the time spent at McDonnell Douglas in California, life at Atlas, indeed in South Africa, proved to be generally dour and dissatisfying. Our general health was a constant cause for concern, with both Thelma and I experiencing unprecedented dental problems and, like many other ex-pats, bronchial difficulties due to the high winds blowing across the mine dumps surrounding the city. Thelma's early warning system had, back in England, been absolutely spot on, for one had to search very hard to find a sense of humour in the middle of the Transvaal. Anything for public consumption such as film entertainment, TV or news distribution was strictly censored. Television was in its infancy in South Africa during the mid-1970s but having appeared on a show called *Specialist* I found myself a minor celebrity (yes, it was that bad) – at least in the area where we lived. Fame is fleeting, however, and the greeting in local shops 'I saw you on TV last night, have a 10 per cent discount' must have lasted all of a couple of days. The programme was based on the British *Mastermind* series and similarly consisted of four contestants each answering questions on their specialist subjects, followed by a number on general knowledge. I had chosen Aircraft and Aviation Personalities of the Second World War, which in hindsight I should have restricted to one or the other. I still managed to come second after the specialist round but dropped to third position by the finish. Not a brilliant result, but at least it enabled me to sample the acid test of intensive questioning while under a spotlight in the dreaded black chair. Now where had I experienced that before? I was particularly aware of not wanting to 'freeze', as does happen even with accredited world experts, but it was said that I acquitted myself fairly well and didn't let the side down.

Many immigrants found that life in the Republic fell short of their expectations. The coastal cities – Cape Town, Durban and Port Elizabeth – being largely populated by English-speaking white South Africans, were naturally more in tune with new arrivals from England, but the Transvaal was Boer (farmer) country where anti-British feeling was often barely concealed. After visiting the Museum of Natural History in Pretoria we decided this was hardly surprising, for it revealed the extent of persecution and concentration camp misery inflicted by British forces on the Boer families just seventy-five years earlier. Two subsequent world wars had made no direct impact on the area and those early hardships had hardened into opinions that were simply passed on to later generations. It was not difficult to see why, after having determined to create an aircraft industry within an Afrikaans-speaking area, the Brits were needed but certainly not welcomed with open arms.

I could never quite get used to the black boy who sat outside my office, whistling all the time while cleaning waste bins with wire wool. Every half an hour or so he would enquire if I wanted tea, but there is only so much one can drink and it was almost embarrassing to keep on refusing his offer. His job, however, was far better than that of the gang of convicts chained together on the lawn outside, cutting the grass with sheep shears.

Summer on the High Veld between October and March brought with it a predictable weather pattern. Each day began with a beautiful, cloudless blue sky, but by late afternoon there would be an ominous build-up of thunderclouds before individual lightning storms surrounded Johannesburg and hailstones descended, on occasions the size of golf balls. Regardless of whether the storms were a ten-minute affair or went on for hours they never failed to be spectacular. On three occasions when we visited the Wanderers cricket ground, rain of monsoon intensity cut play short by a couple of hours.

South African fielding was in a class apart from anything I had ever seen in England. This was shown to marked effect when a 'rebel' tour of the Republic came to the Wanderers, and included such renowned players as Australia's Greg Chappell and England's spinner Phil Edmonds. I marvelled at the difference in the teams' fielding commitments, and especially the South Africans' use of the sliding stop on a rock-hard boundary surface. It is interesting to speculate now, in light of the high professional levels now demanded, how many former England internationals would have met the present squad's fielding performance and fitness requirements. But I digress.

I discovered that several people who had come over to join Atlas before I did had quickly decided that life in Africa was definitely not for them. One can only presume that they had left a return route open that enabled them to quickly pick back up the threads of life in the UK that they had left behind. That had certainly not been an option for us. Having cut the ties of employment and schooling, and effectively being of no fixed abode, we simply had to make things work. Once in our new home, we had soon been subjected to black Africans wanting to do the domestic chores, work in the garden or clean the pool etc. Never having had any assistance on the home front before we had tended to turn it all down, but the neighbouring white families made it clear that doing one's own menial tasks wasn't the 'done thing' and deprived the black Africans of an income. Whichever way we looked, the disparities brought about by apartheid were evident and we felt far from comfortable having to turn a blind eye. I was also coming under increasing pressure at Atlas to apply for South African citizenship. This, I was told, was essential if I wanted to further my career. After three years or so, and with all these factors pressing upon us, I began to check out the work situation back in the UK. Although I had now gained wide experience, I was beginning to wonder if my range of past appointments would be seen by a future employer as advantageous or those of a technical nomad, unable to settle down. Fortunately, the former proved to be the case.

During my time at Blackburn Aircraft working on the Buccaneer I had had a good deal of contact with a Dorset-based company called Flight Refuelling Ltd, and it was following many job applications and extended long-distance telephone calls that I was offered employment as engineering manager in the firm's aerospace components division. I was required to start within several weeks rather than months and it was decided that I should travel back to England ahead of the family, leaving Thelma to sort out the selling of the house and effects. This turned into a separation period of nearly six months before we all met up again in Paris in late 1979. One problem we had to face back in Britain was the cost of living – over the period we had been away prices had risen enormously in the UK, with mortgage rates now at astronomical levels; in South Africa the rate of inflation had remained entirely static. Although the house we had bought there was attractive and boasted a lovely swimming pool, when it came to selling, the only enquiry we received was from the Anglo-American Mining Company. They told us that if they bought it, the pool would have to be filled in as the employee for whom it would be purchased was not of a sufficiently high rank to warrant such a status feature. A bigger cock and bull story I couldn't imagine, but although we knew that it was simply a means of driving down the asking price, with no other offer in sight we had to accept. Why is it, I wonder, that when wishing to sell a property it's always a buyer's market, but when buying it's the other way round?

11

'FLIGHTS'

W e had always tried to time our various moves so that the girls' long-term schooling would not be seriously affected, but this again proved difficult in practice. Returning from South Africa saw Helen and Sally transfer from a rigid and disciplined educational system to a standard British grammar school; unfortunately, in South Africa the subjects had been taught at a lower level than they were in the UK. Not for the first time our daughters found social integration far from easy since groups already formed don't readily take in newcomers. To offset this problem and to provide additional income, we purchased a large Edwardian house in Boscombe near Bournemouth in order to accommodate the foreign students attending the many language schools nearby. This wasn't a solution that I could contribute much to and it fell to Thelma to ensure that the operation ran smoothly.

When I joined Flight Refuelling Ltd it was still essentially a family-run concern and known to all the locals simply as 'Flights'. My new boss, Graham Marriette, most picturesquely described his engineering team as The Choirboys. Seeing my enquiring expression, he said that this was because they were always being f***ed about by Vickers (sic). Off to a good start, then!

Sir Alan Cobham, the company's founder, world famous for his pioneering route-proving flights and touring air displays in the inter-war period, had died in 1973 leaving his second son Michael firmly in charge as chairman and managing director. The company by then had a title which, though appropriate when first coined in 1934, now suggested a limited product line. This was certainly not the case, for in addition to producing aerial refuelling equipment that had a long gestation period for design and development, separate divisions had been formed to design and manufacture nuclear, electronic and aerospace components. This last division had been set up in 1948, when the so-called ABC Agreement had been signed by the American, British and Canadian authorities to define common standards for equipment passing fuel into or out of aircraft on the ground. Henceforward it was no longer acceptable to incur the risk of fire and explosion which was always present when refuelling an aircraft through individual tank filler caps. All new aircraft designs, except very light models and training machines, now had to embody a single-point pressure refuelling system which ensured proportional distribution between the tanks and the means to automatically shut off the supply when they became full. This decision had a large bearing on Flight Refuelling's future, for with all the Western countries now having to conform to the new requirements, the increased income from the sale of suitable system components became the

Right: Helen (right) and Sally soon after returning from South Africa. Both had to overcome 'classmate reserve', which proved very difficult.

Below: Overwing filling of aircraft fuel tanks carried a severe risk of fire and was superseded by single-point closed circuit systems in 1948.

company's prime source of revenue. This all took place at the same time as the firm's heavy involvement in the Berlin Airlift, when twelve Lancaster and Lancastrian aircraft operating from bases in West Germany ferried almost 7 million gallons of motor spirit and domestic heating oil into the beleaguered city. It also coincided with the invention of the 'probe and drogue' method of aerial refuelling that is still in use by major air forces today.

Until the late 1940s, the transfer of fuel in the air had required specialist refuelling operators in both the tanker and receiver aircraft to trail steel cables until they locked together to secure a physical link. With the tanker manoeuvred above and to one side of the receiver, its refuelling operator hauled the cables on board for disconnecting and the attachment of a fuel hose. This was then pulled down by the receiver's operator and fuel allowed to flow under gravity at a typical rate of 100 gallons per minute. This was both cumbersome and dangerous in bad weather or at night. The advent of 'probe and drogue' provided a simplified method of contact and permitted the pilot of a single-seat aircraft to automatically refuel at a much higher rate while concentrating on controlling his machine. This invention had been largely forced along by enquiries put forward by the United States Air Force, and after a successful 'proof of concept' demonstration in 1949, the Americans sent four B-29 Superfortress bombers and two F-84 Thunderjet fighters over to Tarrant Rushton airfield in Dorset for conversion to the new system. Flight Refuelling's team, however, found that the all-electric B-29 and the thin-winged F-84 presented difficult installation problems and the project ended up greatly over budget and well behind the time allocated. This commercial dilemma was only resolved when the

The Berlin Airlift in 1948–49 saw Flight Refuelling Ltd employ a total of twelve Lancasters and Lancastrians on ferrying domestic heating oil and diesel fuel into the beleaguered city. Two company aircraft were lost, one involving the deaths of all but one of the crew. (Cobham Archive)

Sir Alan Cobham's designers produced the 'probe and drogue' air refuelling system being demonstrated here to a USAF evaluation team in 1949. (Cobham Archive)

rights to manufacture the equipment were sold to the American government for a price equal to the overrun. Though tantamount to selling the family silver, Cobham accepted that there was no alternative and over the next decade concentrated on the RAF and the RN as likely customers for his new system.

Notwithstanding the disastrous financial outcome of the conversion, and the fact that the British Overseas Airways Corporation, after trials over the Atlantic, had shown no serious interest in civil air refuelling, Cobham was still convinced that 'probe and drogue' had a military future. Not least in 1949 when company test pilot Pat Hornidge, flying a Gloster Meteor III, set a world record of twelve hours and three minutes for jet aircraft endurance. The flight was duly terminated when the Meteor's engine oil levels got too low and Hornidge found himself saturated after having, so he thought, safely answered the call of nature. Unfortunately, the 'pee' tube which had been installed for this very purpose had failed to do its job. The tube's vent outlet, which should have been positioned at a point of negative pressure on the fuselage skin in order to suck the tube contents overboard, had been located in an area of positive pressure, the accompanying blow back accounting for the pilot's discomfort. Despite having had his enthusiasm somewhat dampened, Hornidge was particularly pleased to receive many congratulatory telegrams, one of which read: 'Well done, indeed. Ten connections in one day. What a man!'

Following this success, Cobham arranged for the first public demonstration of fuel transfer by this method to take place during the SBAC flying display at Farnborough in 1950. It was also planned for the R/T dialogue between Tom Marks, flying a Lincoln tanker, and Hornidge, the Meteor receiver, to be broadcast over the public address system. All went well until a slight disconnect of the probe from the drogue caused a wave of fuel to wash over the Meteor's windscreen – and Hornidge's forceful expletive to wash over the many thousands watching below. Some time later, at a Paris Air Show, this pair of pilots flew, connected, down the Champs-Élysées at roof height, much to the concern of Sir Alan who envisaged serious repercussions from the French authorities. He needn't have worried, for the following day's French papers were ecstatic in their praise.

Flight Refuelling did, throughout the 1960s, supply 'probe and drogue' systems to the Royal Navy for its carrier-based Scimitars and Sea Vixens, which when equipped with

Company test pilot, Pat Hornidge, flying a Gloster Meteor III, takes fuel on board from Tom Marks's Lancaster over Poole Harbour, during his record twelve-hour jet endurance flight on 7 August 1949. (Cobham Archive)

under-wing refuelling pods operated as 'buddy-buddy' tankers. Conceived by the US Navy, the 'buddy' concept allowed an increase in either range or weapon load by topping up aircraft after take-off; alternatively, returning aircraft running low on fuel, and finding a carrier deck obstructed by a damaged machine, could be 'given a drink' from an aircraft temporarily fitted with a quick attachment refuelling pod.

The Lightning and Javelin were the first RAF fighters to be fitted with receiver probes, albeit mainly for long-range deployment, along with the 'V' bomber force; and 214 Squadron, equipped with Valiants, became the first dedicated tanker unit in 1958. It was, however, a long way off Sir Alan's vision of equipping hundreds of USAF tankers and receivers from a subsidiary company, Flight Refueling (*sic*) Incorporated, already set up in Danbury, Connecticut, for that very purpose.

The system truly proved its worth in 1982, when it provided the means for carrying out long-distance operations during the Falklands War. To add to the existing Victor tanker fleet, an intensive six-week industrial effort by BAE Systems at Woodford, Marshall of Cambridge and Flight Refuelling at Wimborne saw the RAF's Nimrods, Hercules and Vulcans equipped for fuel transfer. Within this period it was found that when tested, systems that had remained unused for many years sprang leaks from couplings that now had dried-out seals. Faced with replacement shortages, it proved necessary to locate components from aircraft already

The Handley Page Victor remained the RAF's standard tanker for thirty years until its retirement in 1993. It played a crucial part in enabling the Vulcan to attack the airfield at Port Stanley during the Falklands War. (Cobham Archive)

'Tell me, who is that *really* interesting person over there?' The author finds the lady is 'perhaps for turning' during her visit to Wimborne.

retired from service. In one case, a refuelling nozzle was removed from a Vulcan in the USAF Museum at Castle Air Force Base in California!

Undoubtedly the most striking example of air refuelling's 'force extending' capabilities was the Black Buck raid by Flight Lieutenant Martin Withers' Vulcan on the airfield at Port Stanley during the Falklands conflict. This required a round trip of 7,800 miles, with eleven Victor tankers progressively refuelling each other, along with the Vulcan on its outbound leg and five tankers being involved on its return. A total of eighteen contacts, all at night and on occasions in appalling weather, saw the transfer of some 500,000lb of fuel, all of which added up to a magnificent logistical and operational achievement.

The company's part in this was recognised on 16 July 1982, when the Rt Hon. Margaret Thatcher paid a visit to the Wimborne factory where she met and talked with a number of employees. I was among the favoured few, but that was more to do with the retractable refuelling probe assembly for the McDonnell Douglas AV-8B (Harrier II) when it was demonstrated to her in the test house. I recall two incidents during the Iron Lady's visit that caused mirth (fortunately fairly silent) and acute embarrassment in more or less equal proportions. The first occurred when the aforementioned probe was extended from its compact, horizontal, retracted position to its impressive full length and at an appreciable angle. While the good lady and her husband were admiring this somewhat phallic extension, 'Beat that, Denis' came forth from some disrespectful wag in a loud whisper that would surely have tested her sense of humour had it carried through the hubbub of surrounding conversation.

Tom Brooke-Smith was the first man to undertake vertical flight in a fixed-wing aircraft. He also nearly caused Prime Minister Margaret Thatcher to crash-land when she was being seated in the chairman's office! (Cobham Archive)

A crowning career fulfilment was the opportunity to fly in the Battle of Britain Flight's Lancaster. This picture shows that flight, as the Lancaster passes over Middle Wallop, affording the author the chance of a lifetime to photograph the Flight's Hurricane and Spitfire Mk XIX (see overleaf).

The second incident could have had more serious repercussions for, when invited to sit and sign the visitors' book in Michael Cobham's office, ex-Shorts chief test pilot Tom Brooke-Smith, then the company's public relations executive, mistimed his attentiveness and pulled away the chair just as she tried to sit down. This was not a career-enhancing move and although 'Brookie' was mortified at seeing her fall, Mrs Thatcher having caught the edge of the desk immediately recovered her composure and claimed the blame for herself. I'm not entirely certain that Michael Cobham agreed with her, but her recognition of Wimborne's contribution was unaffected and went down well with the workforce.

Now what could be better than that: Hurricane on the starboard wing (above), Spitfire on the port side (below)?

In mentioning just a few of the company's milestone events, I would be remiss if I didn't remark on the significant contribution made by the aerospace components division to Concorde's technical success. This may be underlined by the fact that for a typical transatlantic flight, some 65 tons of fuel had to be received on board, transferred, controlled, cooled and heated, pressurised and measured by equipment that included 200 separate assemblies and 1,800 pipe couplings, all produced at Wimborne. A fair contribution, one might say, though I recall one French lady who wasn't too impressed. While on stand duty at a Paris Air Show in the early 1980s, she appeared with a small boy, and pointing to a company leaflet describing our contribution to Concorde, asked if she could have one. 'Certainement, Madame,' said I, pleased to be of assistance. However, having not even moved off the stand, she bent down and wrapped the child's dripping hamburger in it. With a 'Merci, Monsieur' she made an unhurried departure, and brought broad smiles to those watching. I doubt she would have done it with a French publication.

By the 1980s, Flight Refuelling Ltd had already taken over the Saunders Valve Company and now held a virtual monopoly on the supply of fuel system components for British aircraft. It was, therefore, able to assist the RAF's Battle of Britain Memorial Flight when the sole flying Lancaster, PA 474, was due to be grounded because specially shaped rubber seals in the fuel cock-boxes, originally supplied by Saunders, had deteriorated and replacements were no longer available. Having obtained one of the damaged items to use as a template, Flight Refuelling's rubber shop was able to fabricate three replacement sets which should outlast the rest of the airframe. After co-ordinating this salvage operation I was offered a flight in the Lancaster from Coningsby to Yeovilton, which to the envy of many I had little difficulty in accepting. Nor did I turn down later opportunities for two further flights in that iconic aircraft. I never regarded these experiences in cash value terms, but noting that a flight today in the Canadian-restored Lancaster costs £400, it put my good fortune into a sizeable financial perspective.

My tenure as engineering manager of this division ended after four years when I became the head of engineering services in the company, an appointment which took account of the reliability and maintainability, technical publications and reproduction departments. At this time there was an increasing need to comply with a new discipline imported from America, called 'logistics'. It soon became a key element in the company's bid to win the retractable refuelling probe contract for the McDonnell Douglas (McAir) AV-8B. The extensive documentation it required to identify equipment costs throughout its service life formed a significant part of the technical and commercial proposals to fit wing-mounted refuelling pods on the same company's KC-10 tanker. Technical discussions required frequent visits to St Louis and Los Angeles, and one trip that remains forever in my mind involves the days when the company's personnel flew on the now-defunct British Caledonian Airways.

This airline did wonders for the ego, as it provided transportation to and from the hotel in a tinted-window stretch limo. On one occasion I had attended a meeting at one of McDonnell Douglas's offices and was travelling to another, where the limo was meant to be waiting to take me back to the airport. On entering the approach road to the office, I noticed a scuffle going on outside the main reception area; I sidestepped the melee and went inside only to find an extremely agitated driver clutching a cup of coffee. It turned out that he had turned up slightly ahead of schedule and after parking the limo had gone inside to see if I had arrived. The limo had then been hijacked and chased by the McAir security guards, who just managed to intercept it before it could join the busy traffic on the main highway. What I had seen as an undignified scrap was the apprehension of a member of the hijacking team who had been attempting to escape. This jolly adventure was duly capped when, with me finally seated and ready for the off, a firm hand appeared on the windscreen and its owner intoned that a felony had been committed and that the car was now impounded. To his great credit, the driver responded with high indignation, saying that he had to get the commander to the airport.

'Is that right, commander?' enquired the faceless wonder, whose chest I seemed to be addressing from inside the car. My smart 'it certainly is' was met with a smiling face, a salute and 'OK, have a nice day, sir. Go on through!' Having finally got moving, my driver, Ib Weinberg, informed me that he had not only worked for the well-known country and western singer Merle Haggard, he also gave body massages when required! Clearly, here was a man of versatile talents and I told him that this was good to know. The strange sequel to this bizarre event is that when I returned a couple of weeks later, this weird individual turned up again. When I mentioned our earlier adventure, he said he did not remember a thing about it, which left me seriously wondering if I had dreamed the whole thing. That's California for you.

Meetings in America can be very intimidating experiences, until one knows what to expect. It was never Flight Refuelling's policy to send over large teams of people, and even if they had, the cost of frequent travelling would have soon proved prohibitive. Our relatively meagre representations often felt like General Custer's small band in the face of the large numbers of specialists invariably brought in by McDonnell Douglas. To be outnumbered five to one was commonplace and it required our people to be good at thinking on their feet. As indicated in my earlier comments on working practices in the US, with so many people engaged on individually narrower fronts, it was inevitable that when we were called upon to make any kind of comment, it was perceptively interrogated from several different viewpoints. Woe betide any visitor who was not well versed in his given subject, for, not unlike the Senate or congressional investigations that always appear so heavily populated, one could lose credibility very quickly. Not everybody's cup of cawfee!

I faced some severe pressure on one occasion when, during the second Gulf War, I was sent over on my own to attend a series of meetings at the Pentagon. The need for this had arisen quickly, when the USAF decided there might be a case for equipping certain of their aircraft with the latest 'probe and drogue' refuelling systems. Since the late 1940s the USAF had employed the rival 'boom' system devised by Boeing. Although capable of passing higher flow rates than the British system, it required a dedicated operator in the tanker to steer a long telescopic probe into a mating receptacle in the receiver. Once connected, it then formed a rigid link between the two aircraft that was unpopular with many pilots and limited the tanker to refuelling one receiver at a time. With the war then in full swing, and interoperability between different nations' air forces then a paramount requirement, Flight Refuelling's digitally controlled system was seen as offering far more flexibility. The Americans needed to know all about the system and especially its reliability

The Falconet was a subsonic aerial target designed at Flight Refuelling Ltd for use by the British Army for gunnery training. Jet powered, and mounted on a tethered trolley, it raced round a circular track until it achieved flying speed. It also formed part of the company's bid to supply targets to Saudi Arabia, which proved to be my last full-time involvement with Flight Refuelling before health problems forced early retirement. (Cobham Archive)

and maintainability. All the RAF personnel who could have provided fault, defect and mean time between failure figures were either out in the Gulf or simply not available, and it was a case of my putting together, at very short notice, a hopefully convincing presentation.

The Pentagon, with its massively long corridors, is a daunting place in which to find one's way, and when finally faced with a legion of pencil-tapping colonels sensing easy meat, my 'it's nice to see all of you here this morning, gentlemen' might have seemed a little forced. The initial large gathering soon split into a number of smaller, more manageable, working parties and I returned home feeling I had done all I could to further the company cause. My effort was but a minor influence in the USAF's decision to retain the 'boom' system for its receiver aircraft, but to employ 'probe and drogue' wing pods and a boom system on its tankers for international operations.

A footnote to this experience is that this visit coincided with my urgent need to visit a hairdresser. I mentioned this on arrival to our US representative, Frank Morien, who assured me that he knew just the place for me to get a quick trim before facing my military inquisitors. I was already through the Pentagon's security barriers when he pointed out the hairdressing establishment he had in mind. There, already completely bald in my view, sat a row of impassive US Marines awaiting further defoliation. This was most certainly not for me and after recovering from the shock of my narrow escape, I saw Morien fast disappearing to safety down a long corridor, leaving me to retain my relatively long-haired appearance.

While on the subject of Anglo-American co-operation, one may recall the political scandal in 1986–87 that became known as the Westland Affair. This revolved around the Westland Helicopter company's fight for survival and its immediate need for additional funding. Bitter divisions arose within Mrs Thatcher's government as to whether the American United Technologies group or a European rival should provide the rescue package. The offer from across the Atlantic brought with it the attractive inducement of allowing Sikorsky Black Hawk helicopters to be built under licence as the WS-70 at Yeovil. Not surprisingly, this won the approval of the Westland Board and Mrs Thatcher's Cabinet. There were, however, two senior Cabinet members – the defence secretary, Michael Heseltine, and the industry secretary, Leon Brittan – who, strongly wedded to European integration, promptly offered their resignations. In the event, the outbreak of the Gulf War brought political and financial difficulties that resulted in the withdrawal of Sikorsky's support and the rescinding of the licence to build the Black Hawk. But all was not lost on the collaboration front, because Westland and the Italian company Agusta, having earlier worked together to produce the Sioux light helicopter, teamed up as European Helicopter Industries to develop and produce the EH 101. Westland later became a fully owned Agusta company,

Returning to more familiar ground, Flight Refuelling became increasingly involved in drone (unmanned) aircraft conversions and towed target projects. This led to the production of a range of small aircraft that could serve as expendable targets or as more sophisticated reconnaissance vehicles for artillery support. In late 1991 the company was asked by the Saudi Arabian government to submit a bid that covered the supply of high- and low-speed targets. The quotation had to cover not only the supply of the aircraft, but all aspects of support, from the spares and ground equipment required to training, technical publications etc. – whatever was necessary to operate in 'quick set-up' desert conditions and also from ships at sea. My task was to co-ordinate the logistics input to the bid. It was also considered a good idea for me to go out with our sales representative and get a feel for the local conditions. Although I had spent a fair amount of time in different countries and companies abroad, I still felt a total novice when first exposed to the Middle Eastern business environment.

Upon arriving in Riyadh I was ushered into a strange world of white-clad sheikhs who were apparently all related in some way to the royal family. The meetings went on for several days, but never seemed to get anywhere; one 'cousin' would always wish to defer to another whom I would meet, if lucky, the following day. As it turned out, Flight Refuelling was not awarded the contract, which was instead won by Lockheed. The general feeling back at Wimborne was that Lockheed, which had supplied similar equipment to the Saudis in the past, was a foregone winner and that Flight Refuelling's invitation to bid was merely a ploy to drive down the American company's price. I could well believe it, but such is the nature of commercial warfare – you have to be in the race to stand a chance of winning!

It was while in Bahrain that I first had the feeling of being unwell, but the sensation soon passed and I returned to Heathrow the following day. Two days later, on 1 December 1991, while visiting friends in Bristol, I suffered a severe heart attack. With my mother's death a month earlier and being burgled a couple of weeks after my attack, it wasn't the best lead-up to Christmas. Later judged by the company doctor as being 'no longer fit for purpose', I entered early retirement in April 1992. Then aged 59, I naturally wondered what the future held, but though I couldn't see it at the time, I was about to embark on a very different, but perhaps the most enjoyable, part of my career. I have since thought it likely that the stress of preparing the logistics quotation contributed to my hospitalisation. Luckily I made a good recovery, but I became aware of how many industrial casualties end up far less fortunate. One may wonder about the number of workers on 'important' projects who have their health and marriages seriously affected only to find out later that their efforts had produced little of lasting value. Such unfortunate outcomes are, of course, inevitable and are by no means confined to the aerospace industry. The conclusion may therefore be drawn that if a solution to worrying about work exists, no one has yet discovered it.

12

LIFE IN THE OLD DOG YET

L ife's expenses never cease and in 1992, at nearly 60 and facing an uncertain health situation, what was one to do? Though my options seemed few, it dawned on me one day that perhaps the answer was staring me in the face. The problem was to convince other people, in this case Michael Cobham, then chairman of the FR Group (Flight Refuelling Ltd being its main company), that I could write the organisation's history and create an archive. I recall that my first acquaintance with him after just starting at the company had not been auspicious. Having submitted a draft company capability brochure to him for general approval, I was called into his office for what I thought would be a 'yes, good idea, go ahead'. What I unexpectedly received was furious condemnation for misplaced commas and hyphens etc. My stuttered explanation that it was merely a draft for his approval did little to dilute what turned out to be a fearsome rollicking. Fortunately for me, I subsequently had social contact with him outside the company, for at that time he was president of the Royal Aeronautical Society's Christchurch branch and I had become chairman (later to succeed him as president). It was through unashamedly leaning on this relationship that I eventually persuaded him to let me take on the task of recording the company's history. Even so, he expressed concern that I was not a professional writer and, as he was still actively engaged as company chairman, would find it difficult to devote the time necessary to contributing and editing whatever I might put together from other sources. But other factors were working in my favour. Not only was the 60th anniversary of Flight Refuelling Ltd's formation coming up in 1994, but the announcement of a major name change from FR Group plc to Cobham plc was scheduled to coincide with this event.

Such happenings are always warily regarded within the City and Michael Cobham was certainly preoccupied with what effect this change would have on the Group's share price. After some discussion, the Board decided that something had to be done to provide a suitable commemoration and I was asked to provide three sample chapters of what was to become *In Cobhams' Company*. These fortunately met with approval and I set about producing the goods. Michael Cobham made me aware that Sir Arthur Marshall, the head of the rival firm Marshall of Cambridge, was also working on an autobiography due to be published around the time of the Cobham plc announcement. His wish not to be upstaged by this gave further impetus to my task and it required a fair number of gin and tonics on Saturday mornings in the boss's office before we hammered out the final result. Michael was most insistent that in the book's title the apostrophe went after the 's', for as he put it, 'the old man ran the

The re-branding changeover took place in 1994 and saw Sir Michael Knight take over from Sir Michael Cobham as chairman. (Cobham Archive)

company for thirty years but then, so did I, so make damn sure that this is well reflected in what you write.' 'Point already noted, sir. Cheers!'

Taking on this task allowed me to name drop my way into many privileged situations. For example, it was most useful to be able to call up service chiefs or captains of industry and preface my enquiry with, 'Michael Cobham has suggested I contact you, regarding ...' Such was his standing in the industry that co-operation was willingly given by everyone I approached. I might have bent the rules a little by using this tactic to obtain flights on the Victor, Hercules, VC10 and TriStar tankers and receivers to get the 'feel of things' during typical air refuelling missions, but the opportunities were too good to miss. As, indeed, was the chance to wing-walk – or at least stand – on Cadbury's Crunchie Boeing Stearman Kaydet when I was preparing a later book on the inter-war touring flying displays led by Sir Alan Cobham's Flying Circus. This was an entirely different experience and I thought at the time that, being then aged 67, I might have been the oldest to undertake such a flight. I was soon disabused of that idea for a gentleman in his nineties, and another minus one leg, had already taken part in similar ventures. No doubt several others have now long overtaken my imagined claim to fame.

When Cobham plc came into being, Air Chief Marshal Sir Michael Knight succeeded (the by then) Sir Michael Cobham as chairman. Perhaps one interesting point to record here is that on the day that Sir Michael Cobham's knighthood was announced, I was in his office and he asked me if I had read the day's papers. When I said that I had, he replied, 'Well, not well enough apparently' and pushed across a copy of *The Times* which announced his appointment. Upon my very genuine reaction of 'Well, well, Sir Michael', he interrupted any further comment by saying: 'That's the first and last time you ever call me by that title.' So Michael it remained, an indication, perhaps, of the warmth and understanding that existed between us until his death in 2004.

Boardroom personality clashes occasionally caused me to be awkwardly placed, and none more so than when Sir Michael asked me to rewrite contributions prepared by senior executives for the company's Annual Reports. One can understand that this did not go down too well in certain quarters. My usual diplomatic tactic was to explain to the aggrieved parties that it wasn't the document's content that was at issue, it was just that I wrote in the chairman's style which he felt more comfortable with. I don't think this impressed those affected and it often left me feeling like a Wimbledon tennis ball in having to change direction pretty rapidly.

In writing *In Cobhams' Company* it was frequently necessary to obtain the opinions of aviation personalities, such as Alex Henshaw, Brian Trubshaw, John Cunningham, Peter Twiss, Sir Michael Beetham or Lettice Curtis, to name but a few. The request to prepare an acceptance speech for Sir Michael to deliver, following his father's posthumous induction into the San Diego Aerospace Museum's Hall of Fame, was for me a particular highlight. I must admit that although a prized, social, black-tie event, two incidents occurred which threw doubt on the showbiz adage 'it'll be alright on the night'. The music for the evening was to be provided by the United States Marine Band, which, though stationed in San Diego, had managed to get lost en route to the prestigious hotel. Having been billed as a prime feature on the evening's programme, no one could understand where they had got to, but there was a collective sigh of relief when they finally appeared. The second source of amusement, to Thelma and I at least, was the master of ceremonies, Hollywood actor Cliff Robertson's frequent disappearance into the wings. We assumed that he was either incontinent or in urgent need of liquid refreshment; we later found out that he didn't like to be seen on stage wearing glasses, yet he needed them to quickly read his next set of lines. Such is the price of fame.

Sir Mike Knight possesses an outgoing personality and seems to know the leading lights of every organisation he comes into contact with, if indeed he isn't already heading it himself. The Buccaneer Aircrew Association, to which we both belong and of which he is president, is perhaps a good example. With both of us having a keen sense of aviation history, he and I got on very well and together, during his chairmanship of Cobham plc, we delivered a series of lectures around the country. These usually took the theme of Cobham and, for example, the Blackburn Aircraft Company at Brough, de Havilland at Hatfield or Avro at Woodford. I conducted much of the research and provided the outline text, while Sir Mike delivered the presentations with his natural authority and witty asides and experiences. It was during the Question and Answer sessions afterwards that, despite his being but four months my senior in age, he often referred to me as his amazingly youthful-looking father. My riposte was that later years unfortunately take their toll and that although he had got the youthful-looking bit right, had he traded 'father' for 'knowledgeable colleague' he would have been closer to the mark – this never failed to produce a laugh.

Many doors seemed to open at this time, for not only had I now become Cobham plc's official consultant archivist and historian, I was frequently being called upon to give talks on a variety of aviation subjects. With *In Cobhams' Company* proving popular, my writing confidence greatly increased and I found myself producing a succession of aviation titles. This, I must add, was largely due to Thelma's encouragement and her ability to ring-fence my wandering prose to good effect.

POSTSCRIPT

The British aircraft industry that I worked in has now totally disappeared. No longer can one find more than the odd reference to the original pioneering firms such as Fairey, de Havilland, Shorts, Avro or Handley Page in today's list of companies. Complete Hawk aircraft are no longer assembled at the old Blackburn factory in Brough, and the cessation of manufacturing now brings the strong possibility of the plant no longer having any association with aviation. Should this occur, the final nail will, symbolically, have been driven into the old industry's coffin. Even Flight Refuelling Ltd, once held in high regard not only for its products, but also for the uniquely welcoming voices of its switchboard girls, has lost its original identity: it is now the mission equipment division of the albeit successful Cobham plc.

It was, unfortunately, a painful necessity that the long list of British companies that produced highly individual brands of aeroplanes and engines had to provide a more critical mass. Even before the war, too many firms were chasing too few contracts where the hope of sizeable production runs could never be realised. The need for increased aircraft manufacture between 1939 and 1945 kept many companies in business with subcontracted work, but the problem soon reappeared in the years after the war. As pointed out earlier, perhaps the most glaring examples of post-war company folly were the Brabazon and the Princess flying boat. Both were expensive and misguided airliner projects that produced visually elegant and technical masterpieces which flew straight on to the commercial scrapheap. No longer was it a prime requirement to cater for the privileged social or civil service elite in pre-war-style luxury. Time and passenger necessities had moved on. Neither the companies involved, nor indeed the country, could afford to pour money down the drain for such little return. But these lessons were not absorbed overnight, and the emerging strength of the mainland European aviation companies offered a growing threat to Britain's supposed supremacy.

Today, the country's streamlined and slimmed-down workforce sees our brightest aeronautical brains engaged on some challenging projects. The advanced processes involved at Filton and Broughton in the production of wings for the Airbus series of airliners provide positive proof of the skills available within the British aerospace industry. However, such is the changing nature of international politics and the emergence of foreign industrial expertise that Great Britain can never afford to rest upon its laurels. The threat of major work transfer overseas is forever the unwanted guest at the banquet. Much work is also being devoted to unmanned aircraft for military use where the sizes range from full-scale machines, as already proven in Afghanistan, down to hummingbird-sized (if not smaller) intelligence gatherers. While relatively small drones are now being considered for crowd and traffic surveillance by police authorities, the introduction of drone airliners into civil operations, though technically feasible even now, may well be long delayed until disparate airworthiness bodies around the world agree upon safe rules for their operation. Consider, for example, the legal implications of a pilotless airliner registered in Britain, operated by a company possibly based in Europe, carrying a full passenger complement of, say, Asian people that crashes in yet another country. The accident investigation and insurance implications are already immense for manned aircraft, but there would be added complications for an aircraft under remote control. It may also be that the general flying public are not comfortable without a reassuringly handsome captain up front. Houston, I think we have a problem!

Advances in avionic and electronic equipment that incorporate highly sophisticated sensors now confirm that the value of an air vehicle lies in the 'package' being carried. My early days in the industry led me to think the opposite was true, with the aeroplane being the valuable bit and its contents of secondary importance. We live and learn! What makes today's marketplace so much more competitive is the pace at which so many other countries, China and India being prime examples, have accelerated their own design and manufacturing skills. Foreign growth and the enormous costs involved in major new projects make more international co-operation inevitable, and perhaps even desirable, assuming the various European debt crises can be resolved. There are, of course, certain countries whose technical capabilities are unquestionably excellent but whose financial stability is woeful. No prizes for guessing which fall into that category, but I would be surprised if either Italy or Spain (forget Greece, as it doesn't have an aviation industry) feature in any large collaborative projects in the near future.

Many of my comments have been made with the benefit of that soothing balm 'hindsight', and I fully appreciate that complicated and far-reaching decisions have to be made regarding equipment for service use many years ahead. However, as I write this, the latest teeth-gritting chapter is being played out regarding the Lockheed Martin Joint Strike Fighter. In the first instance the variant approved by the Labour government for the Royal Navy was the F35 B which, like its Harrier predecessor, possesses Short Take Off and Vertical Landing capabilities. This model, having a smaller fuel capacity than the more conventional F35 C, has in consequence a reduced range and carries fewer weapons. But it is a much cheaper option and one Britain's coalition government has had to revert to after its defence minister, Dr Liam Fox, initially cancelled Labour's choice in favour of the F35 C. Despite the political embarrassment of this major U-turn, there was simply no room for financial manoeuvre, when the extra cost and delay incurred in installing catapult launch and arrested landing gear into the new carriers to accommodate it, was set against the reduced service budget. As a taxpayer who has watched billions of pounds disappear to little useful effect over the years, I am encouraged that a brave but sensible decision has been made; but I remain unconvinced that things are about to fundamentally change when requirement definition, equipment provision and Treasury restrictions remain forever at odds with each other.

Harold Macmillan, when asked by a journalist what he thought was most likely to blow a government off course, replied: 'Events, dear boy, events.' And so it is with long-range procurement of equipment for any armed services. One has only to look at the decision to scrap the Nimrod MRA 4, an aircraft not unlike Concorde in so far as it attracted intense and controversial debate throughout its long gestation period. At the time its cancellation was announced in the 2010 Strategic Defence Review, the MRA 4 programme was £789 million over budget and running nine years late. There was also the small matter of several hundred design non-compliances, along with aerodynamic issues, system problems and flying control concerns still to be resolved. Add to that the RAF and Royal Navy stating that higher priority had to be given to fast jets and frigates for maritime patrol work, and it becomes clear that the initial procurement planners never stood a chance.

The above brief reference to Concorde brings to mind another instance of how things change. In 2008 I was requested to co-ordinate a display of historic aircraft from the Shuttleworth Collection at Old Warden to represent an Alan Cobham Flying Circus at the SBAC Exhibition at Farnborough. In relation to the flying content, I paid a visit to Concorde's ex-chief test pilot, Brian Trubshaw, who was then a member of the committee controlling the show's flying activities. During our discussion I requested a copy of his career CV to assist my general write-up for the programme. 'Haven't got one to hand, old man,' said he. 'But chat to the PR department at Filton; they will have something.'

When I did contact the BAE Systems people they regarded my enquiry with some surprise and professed not to know who Brian Trubshaw was! To me, Concorde and Trubshaw are an inseparable pair and this incident just underlined the metamorphosis of the industry from what I used to know to what it has now become – a bland business stripped of design and flying personalities. Just to further illustrate my point, during the early 1950s, and prior to the 'aircraft industry' becoming the 'aerospace industry', it was not uncommon for the general public to link test pilots and designers with the latest technology and spectacular events. Neville Duke and John Derry, along with their respective mounts the Hawker Hunter and de Havilland 110, were two pilots that perhaps best typified the annual Farnborough Air Show. George Edwards, too, was a well-known name associated with the Viscount airliner. These, and others, were individuals whose skills were familiar to large sections of the British population. Today, few people – even within aviation – could name the chief test pilot of Airbus Industries. This may well be deliberate, as the personality cult has been squeezed out in favour of the corporate image, plus there are relatively few new types of aircraft in the skies.

In fairness, test pilots in the early post-war period, who were at the sharp end of development when probing the mystical sound barrier, were deservedly awarded much industrial and public acclaim. Today's test pilots are a different breed: no doubt they would have been equally willing to explore those early, dangerous frontiers, but nowadays they are mainly required to confirm results already confidently predicted by computer analysis. Yet flight test programmes still carry a measure of uncertainty and call for a quiet degree of aircrew courage which I most certainly respect.

I am far from qualified to make crystal-ball projections regarding the way forward for the aerospace industry in the UK. Like every other average citizen, I have no access to the true, unpublished facts that the political, military and industrial teams have to take into account when making major decisions affecting the future. What I would predict with reasonable conviction is that they will be eventually castigated for having got the right answer to the wrong problem and for a price that is no longer affordable. 'Twas, it seems, ever thus and forever will be, Amen!

* * *

This book began with recollections of my boyhood years spent in Bridlington. Now, with my journey's tale almost done, and in the wake of our annual visit up north to where it all began, it strikes me that a parallel can be drawn between my home town's fortunes and those of the aircraft industry. For over twenty years a bitter debate has raged as to whether the construction of a yachting marina would provide a money-making attraction for the town. This has gone hand in hand with other entrepreneurial schemes to regenerate the town centre. Expensive consultations as to the size and likely success of such a harbour have so far come to nought, primarily because it has proved impossible to find a developer willing to support such aspirations. These long-standing discussions have also had to take in many other considerations, such as the impact on local fishing and pleasure craft owners, and the need to modify piers protected by Listed Building laws. Whether or not there would be a sufficient number of boat owners wishing to use such a facility, when existing docks at both Hull and West Hartlepool have already been converted to provide large (and questionably profitable) berthing capacities, remains a big unknown. This is where a comparison with the problems besetting aviation becomes apparent. In both cases, far-sighted men and women have seen what the future *could* hold, but their projects have been thwarted by a mixture of resistance to change, lack of common sense and, inevitably, a shortage of finances, especially in times of recession. There are, nevertheless, many instances of hard-won success and I have already made reference to some of the winners and losers in the aviation world. Where Bridlington is concerned, it can point with great pride to the beautiful restoration of The Spa complex and to the north- and south-side pedestrian areas facing the sea. But whether it be Bridlington or Blackburns at Brough (it doesn't come naturally to my ancient mind to regard the factory as anything else), 'events, dear boy, events' will always make project life difficult. I wonder if the pyramid builders, or those at Stonehenge, had such problems to overcome. I would be surprised if they hadn't!

APPENDIX I

This amusing correspondence relating to the accuracy of published data concerning Tarrant Rushton Airfield took place in 1953.

COPY

G.R.

From:- No. 1 A.I.D. Unit, Royal Air Force, Ruislip.

To:- The S.A.T.C.O. Air Traffic Control, Tarrant Rushton.

Date:- 28th April, 1953.

Ref:- AID/1010/45/EAV

APPROACH AND LANDING CHARTS:- ELEVATION

It has been brought to our notice by Air Ministry, Works 8, who operate in conjunction with Ministry of Civil Aviation that during a recent survey the elevation of Tarrant Rushton differs from the one printed in pilots Handbook.

The elevation as printed is 300, whilst that of the Survey Team is 301ft.

It is therefore requested that you confirm one or the other of these elevations, and inform this unit accordingly.

(Sgd.) C.D. HALLETT P/O
for Squadron Leader, Commanding,
No. 1 A.I.D. Unit, Ruislip.

From:- Royal Air Force, Tarrant Rushton.

To:-   No. 1 A.I.D. Unit, Royal Air Force, Ruislip.

Date:- 15th May, 1953.

Ref:- GRM/55/Air

APPROACH AND LANDING CHARTS – ELEVATION OF TARRANT RUSHTON AIRFIELD

1.   Reference is made to your AID/1010/345/NAV dated 28th April, 1953, requesting confirmation of one of the alternatives, 300 or 301 feet as the correct elevation of the above-mentioned airfield.

2.   It is pointed out that, owing to the sinusoidal characteristics of the runways, temperature changes throughout the year cause the elevation of the touch-down points to vary from their mean values roughly in accordance with the equation

$$d = \pm\ 6'' \cos 2\pi t$$

where 'd' is the vertical displacement from the mean position in inches and 't' is the epoch in fractions of a year measured from the average date of maximum displacement due to low temperature. This date is fixed as 14th February. The plus or minus sign depends on whether the touch-down position is above or below the mean elevation on that date. (Owing to the thermal inertia of runways, diurnal variations are tentatively considered negligible.)

3.   It will be seen from the above equation that the total range of elevation of the runways is one foot, neglecting very slow secular changes consequential upon Weber's Theory of Continental Drift, and it is advanced that this difference possibly accounts for the ambiguity in the elevations recorded.

4.   The operational aspect, however, must not be ignored and attention is directed to the following facts regarding the use of the current standard height reference instrument of the Royal Air Force: viz, the Mark XIV Sensitive Altimeter:-

   (a) This instrument is calibrated to an average atmosphere (the I.C.A.N. atmosphere) and prevailing weather conditions can, and in fact often do, cause departures from the standard which, in turn, causes the true altitude to differ from that indicated by more than one foot.

   (b) Furthermore, the face of this instrument is not graduated to read so small an interval as one foot.

   (c) Finally, even if the above two points were eliminated as factors in the case – a most unlikely contingency – there is no pilot who can fly an aircraft within a height band of a thickness of one foot.

5.   In addition, your attention is directed to the 1:500,000 scale map of Southern England and Wales, G.S.G.S. 4072, first edition, with air information as at May, 1951, supplied by the Ministry of Defence, J.I.B.5, wherein it is written that the height of Tarrant Rushton airfield is 255 feet.

6.   In view of the foregoing, therefore, and the fact that there
is in any event a variation of 60 feet between the highest
and lowest points on the airfield, it is humbly and yet quite
confidently submitted that not even the most pernickety of
pilots, either service or civilian, would be unduly concerned
over a possible error of 12 inches in the advertised height
of Tarrant Rushton Aerodrome.

7.   If however it is maintained that an error of 12 inches in
the published height of the airfield constitutes a hazard to
the safe operation of aircraft from Tarrant Rushton, it is
recommended, in order to save the taxpayer the cost of a further
and more comprehensive survey, that the greater height i.e.
301 feet be accepted as standard.

APPENDIX II

fter delivering a lecture to the Royal Aeronautical Society's Boscombe Down branch one evening, I was introduced to Mr and Mrs Peter French. Knowing that I hailed from Bridlington, Peter, an ex-RAF officer, regaled me with this Yorkshire tale. Unwilling to abbreviate his descriptive account of what turned out to be a white-knuckle experience I have included it for its local relevance. This is another example of my being 'around at the time' but only becoming aware of the event many years later. Sadly, Peter died in 2008, leaving many test pilot tales untold, but the following is reproduced by kind permission of his wife Olive:

It Started with an Oil Leak

It was wartime in 1944, and all around the world momentous events were changing the course of history. I was, by then, an experienced pilot in the Royal Air Force (having entered the service a year or so before the outbreak of hostilities) and stationed at Lindholme, on the wintry Vale of York in the bleak north-east of England.

On 16 January I prepared to make a routine flight with passengers to St Eval in Cornwall, some 300 miles away. Our aircraft, an elderly Airspeed Oxford, was a versatile, twin-engined, training-cum-transport monoplane of medium size. Built largely of wood, it was noisy and a pig to fly on one engine, but it was reliable and fairly fast. Significantly, it was also fitted with a Lorenz Blind Approach Radio to facilitate landings in poor visibility.

The day of departure dawned fine, with unbroken sunshine which soon burned off the last remnants of overnight fog. By mid-morning, conditions for the flight were as near perfect as could be. Just three minutes before take-off, however, the port engine began to leak oil. This was a potentially time-consuming setback, for, with no standby aircraft available, I had little option but to wait for the machine to be repaired. My impatience mounted as precious minutes ticked by, as I knew that any delay in take-off could have dire consequences if the fog was to return later in the day. A telephone message then announced that St Eval was now fog-bound and I was advised to fly to Weston-super-Mare, some 20 miles south-west of Bristol.

While chasing up the repair, I caught sight of another Oxford, which turned out to be the personal mount of the air officer commanding – the most senior officer on the station.

Nodding towards this immaculate machine, I said half-jokingly to the sergeant in charge of the ground crew, 'What if I took that one instead?' Back came an equally jocular, 'Why not? He's away on leave – he'll never know!' By now fretting with impatience, I rashly decided to chance it.

The sacred aircraft was wheeled out of the hangar, engines started, run up and tested, and I signed the Serviceability Certificate making me solely responsible for the aircraft, its contents and my own neck. I picked up my passengers and, heedless of the consequences, opened up the throttles and roared off down the runway.

We made good time and landed at Weston-super-Mare still in warm sunshine. I had planned an immediate return to Yorkshire, but the summer-like weather, together with an

Flight Lieutenant C.R. 'Peter' French was fortunate to survive a tricky landing near Bridlington. (Mrs Olive French)

An Airspeed Oxford advanced trainer, identical to the aircraft which featured in Peter French's adventure.

immediate need for lunch, overcame my better judgement. I left the aircraft in the care of a ground party and went in search of food – my second mistake of the day.

Before departing I checked the latest weather report. It proved to be far from good, for thick fog was now forecast for the entire country. I took off in haste and set course for Yorkshire. By the time I reached the Midlands, barely halfway to my destination, mile upon mile of dense mist blanketed the ground which glowed pink in the light of the setting sun. But not even the sight of this dented my confidence in being able to handle the situation, as I thought the Lorenz Radio beam would keep me out of trouble.

It was not until I drew near to my home aerodrome that I became aware that all was not well with the Lorenz. The signals in my earphones grew weaker and weaker, and then faded into mind-numbing silence. The cockpit instruments revealed no reason for the failure. Dumbfounded at the loss of my lifeline, I sent out a call to base, but received no reply.

I was now in serious trouble, thousands of feet above the Yorkshire Wolds aboard an aircraft with no working radio aids; there was less than an hour's daylight left and little fuel remaining in the tanks. Only a madman would have attempted to land blindly in the fog. Faced with no alternative I would have to bail out. Simple in theory: fly towards the coast, point the aircraft out to sea, engage autopilot, then jump. But the possibility of ending up in the fog beneath, impaled on a church spire, incinerated by high-voltage electricity cables or even drowned in a river caused me to desperately search for other options.

No wind and thick fog with no gaps brought to mind lessons in meteorology learned long ago. From this urgent mind-searching sprang the germ of an idea. Might it not be possible that air currents, generated by the difference in temperature between the cold land and the relatively warmer sea, could have created holes in the surface of the fog? Perhaps if I were to fly immediately to the nearest coastline, about 60 miles away, I might be fortunate enough to locate such a hole. I glanced at my watch, checked the fuel gauges and looked at the sun, now low in the sky. There was just time to test my theory before approaching darkness drew, what might be, the final curtain. The sun was still shining brightly at the height at which I was flying, but I knew that down at ground level it would soon be dusk. Grimly aware that my fate would be decided within the hour, I altered course and set off for the coast.

The sun was just scraping the western horizon when, some miles ahead, I saw a darker patch with a ragged outline staining the white quilt of fog. With rising hope, I dived headlong towards the middle of the patch and saw, to my immense relief, the black waters of the North Sea.

There was no turning back. I screwed up my courage, put the aircraft into a steep bank, spiralled tightly downwards through the tiny gap in the fog and flattened out just above the waves. It was then that I realised I was flying towards an unbroken wall of towering white cliffs. Adrenalin kicked in and I heaved back on the stick, causing the Oxford to mercifully clear the edge of the monstrous cliffs with but feet to spare. Clearly, I hadn't thought things through too well.

It was much darker over the land, and while my eyes adjusted to the fading light and my heartbeat returned to near normal, I flew just above the treetops, half in and half out of the cloud base, searching for somewhere to put down. The first big field I came to had been newly ploughed, but another nearby was grass covered and at first sight looked promising. But when I flew nearer I saw that its surface was studded with concrete anti-glider-invasion posts. As I circled in the deepening twilight to ponder my next move, I glimpsed the distant headlights of vehicles heading in my direction. While a wheels-up landing on the ploughed field would have been relatively safe, the resulting Court of Inquiry into the cause of the damage would have led to a court martial for having taken the aircraft without permission. The alternative was to attempt a landing with the wheels down, in the near dark, in a field stiff with concrete posts. This would be a tremendous gamble, if not an act of sheer lunacy.

There was no time for second thoughts and I decided to take my chances on the field with concrete posts. With undercarriage down, flaps down, and as slowly as I dared, I brought the Oxford, hanging on the props, low over the hedge. I chopped the throttles and she dropped like a stone on to the ground. Then, using brakes and engines alternately in a life-or-death chicane, I zigzagged violently the length of the field in the wildest ride of my life. By some miracle I escaped crashing into the posts, but my heart raced for many moments with the aircraft bucking until it finally skidded to a standstill. Still unable to believe my good fortune, I sat dazed for a while with the engines ticking over.

My next thought was where to leave the aircraft in safety. Nearby was the dark silhouette of a haystack. My hand was poised ready to blast the port throttle wide open to swing the aircraft towards it, when I spotted, only feet away, another of those damned concrete posts. One moment more and I would have smashed straight into it. That shook me more than all that had gone before, for I could have thrown it all away in one simple act of carelessness, just when I thought the job was done. Sick at the realisation, I taxied the Oxford past the post to the lee of the haystack and switched off the engines. Scarcely had I finished fitting the safety locks to the flying controls when a stream of army vehicles swept into the field and within seconds I was encircled by soldiers.

The young officer in charge treated me with great courtesy, despite having been warned (so I later learned) that I might be a spy. Nevertheless, after a brief interrogation I was placed under close arrest and an armed guard was mounted round the aircraft.

I was taken under escort to the headquarters of a searchlight battery in the village of Grindale, just a couple of miles north of Bridlington. Having just flown in from the North Sea, in wartime, unannounced, and in near darkness late on a foggy winter's day, I was not overly surprised at being treated with suspicion by the army. However, there was a curious twist to this event, for when the army officer telephoned Lindholme to check my story, he was told that a pilot resembling my description had been reported killed that afternoon while flying an Airspeed Oxford, in fog, over the Yorkshire Moors. Orders were therefore given that I had to be retained in close custody until formally identified.

My overnight stay at the searchlight battery was most memorable. The kindness shown to me and the generous hospitality with which I was welcomed into the mess was exceptional. As the evening wore on and the drinks flowed, I discovered that the cliffs over which I had flown were at Bempton near Flamborough Head, which rise 400ft above sea level.

Next morning, an officer from my base arrived and, after identification, I returned with him to Lindholme, wondering what sort of a reception awaited me. Much to my surprise, no disciplinary action was taken – neither then, nor later. Perhaps there was a feeling that I had already paid the price for my foolhardiness! It was still necessary, of course, to return the Oxford back to base. Flying it out appeared the obvious thing to do, so men with tractors ripped out all the concrete posts and smoothed over the holes. Then, because the RAF had a regulation which banned pilots who had made a forced landing from flying their aircraft out again, another pilot was delegated to do the job. He took one look at the field and declared that he was not prepared to chance such a risky take-off. A second pilot was sent, but he too refused to fly the aircraft out. In the end, I was summoned to the flight commander's office and told, 'You put it in, you get it out!' – which was, I suppose, a kind of poetic justice. But getting the Oxford out was not to be a simple matter. Experience had taught me that landing an aircraft in a small field was easier than flying it out again. To succeed, everything had to be exactly right, but here all the odds were stacked against it.

I was flown to Lissett aerodrome and taken by car to the farm at Grindale where my charge lay waiting. One look in daylight told me immediately why the other pilots had refused to take on the job. The available take-off distance was short; much shorter than I recalled on my dusk arrival. This meant that I would have to await strong winds to help lift the aircraft into the air. When the next weather system brought favourable conditions some days later,

I returned to the farm. After engine and airframe checks had been carried out, and the aircraft partly refuelled, I taxied into position for take-off, opened the throttles and hoped for the best. Full of promise, the Oxford charged forward over the tufty grass but the build-up of speed was far too slow. It was soon apparent that I had not a hope of getting airborne before reaching the end of the field. I whipped back the throttles, smacked on the brakes and brought the aircraft to a standstill with little distance to spare. The second attempt was equally unsuccessful – the drag of the wheels sinking into the soft ground slowed the aircraft as surely as if the brakes had been applied; again, I was forced to abort the run.

Determined not to give up without some sort of a fight, I decided as a last resort to try a tactic I had used with great success some years earlier during experiments towing giant tank-carrying gliders with equally huge four-engined bombers. I taxied to the downwind boundary, swung the aircraft round to face the strong wind, then locked on the brakes as hard as I could. Next, I lowered the flaps a little, opened the throttles wide, and rammed the control column hard forward. Slowly the tail lifted. When everything was thundering and juddering 'fit to burst', I suddenly released the brakes. The Oxford leapt forward, and as it hurtled over the grass I hung on, and with all my might willed her, desperately, into the air. The boundary hedge was fast approaching when it dawned on me with sickening certainty that, yet again, I was not going to make it.

In a now-or-never reaction, I jerked back on the control column to lift the landing wheels momentarily from the ground, and then quickly shoved it forward to bounce the aircraft into the air. Twice more I repeated the manoeuvre and with each bounce the aircraft picked up a little more speed. Then, with a last giant leap, she sailed over the hedge.

Back at base, I heard from the officer who had been on duty the evening of my forced landing that I had been expected back by mid-afternoon at the latest. When I had not arrived by nightfall – about the time they calculated I should have run out of fuel – it was automatically assumed that I had crashed in some remote spot while attempting to descend through the fog. The electrician who inspected the Oxford after I had landed at Grindale told me that one of the electrical generators had been switched off. The battery had therefore gone flat, which explained the failure of the Lorenz signals and of my radio transmitter. This was almost certainly done while the aircraft was on the ground at Weston-super-Mare. Whether or not that is a conclusive explanation will never be known; what I do know is that someone came very close to switching off my life when they turned off that switch!

AUTHOR'S NOTE

The field in which Peter French landed at Grindale was no stranger to aircraft movements, for it was there, in the early 1930s, that joyriding air displays headed firstly by Charles Barnard and soon after by Sir Alan Cobham took place. From Peter's description, one can only imagine the piloting skills required of these airborne showmen to undertake passenger-carrying and stunt-flying from such typical short-distance fields up and down the country.

The world-famous aviatrix and Yorkshire heroine Amy Johnson and her husband Jim Mollison were also frequent visitors to this particular field, when visiting Amy's parents and grandparents, who were then living in Bridlington.

The long arm of coincidence is at times amazing. One evening during our May 2012 visit to Bridlington, Thelma and I had dinner at The Trout Inn at Wansford near Driffield. Having returned home and mentioned this in a telephone conversation to Bridlington historian David Mooney, he told me that Winston Churchill had, on occasions during the war, been flown up to Driffield to enjoy the trout fishing and had stayed at this well-known inn. His pilot had been Peter French!

INDEX

Published Works by the Same Author

In Cobhams' Company: Sixty Years of Flight Refuelling Ltd (Dovecote Press, 1994)

Cobham: The Flying Years (The History Press, 1997)

In Dorset's Skies (The History Press, 2000)

In Hampshire's Skies (The History Press, 2001)

Those Fabulous Flying Years: Joy Riding and Flying Circuses Between the Wars (Air-Britain, 2003)

In Wiltshire's Skies (The History Press, 2004)

Highways to the Empire: Long-Distance Flying Between the Wars (Air-Britain, 2006)

100 Years of Advertising in British Aviation (The History Press, 2008)

In Somerset's Skies (Amberley Press, 2010)

Collaborative Works

Various authors, *Faster, Further, Higher: Leading-Edge Aviation Technology since 1945* (Putnam Aeronautical Books, 2002)

Cobham, Sir Alan, *To the Ends of the Earth* (reprint by The History Press, 2002)

Cobham, Sir Alan, *Twenty-thousand Miles in a Flying Boat: My Flight Round Africa* (reprint by The History Press, 2007)

Cruddas, C. & Smart, P., *Cobham 75* (Dovecote Press, 2009, for company use only)